Dogspeak

Dogspeak

How to Understand Your Dog and Help Him Understand You

From the Editors of
Pets part of the family

Edited by Matthew Hoffman

Consultant: Paul McGreevy, B.V.Sc., Ph.D.,
veterinarian and lecturer in animal behavior at
the University of Sydney, Australia

Rodale Press, Inc.
Emmaus, Pennsylvania

Notice

This book is intended as a reference volume only, not as a medical manual. The information given here is designed to help you make informed decisions about your pet's behavior. It is not intended as a substitute for any treatment that may have been recommended by your veterinarian. If you suspect that your pet has a serious behavior problem, we urge you to seek competent help.

Printed in the United States of America on acid free ∞ , recycled paper ♲

Library of Congress Cataloging-in-Publication Data

Dogspeak : how to understand your dog and help him understand you /
  edited by Matthew Hoffman.
      p.   cm. — (Dog care companions)
  Includes index.
  ISBN 1–57954–049–X hardcover
  1. Dogs—behavior. 2. Human-animal communication. I. Hoffman,
Matthew. II. Series.
SF433.D654 1999
636.7'088'7—dc21   98–52352

Distributed to the book trade by St. Martin's Press
2 4 6 8 10 9 7 5 3 1 hardcover

OUR PURPOSE

To explore, celebrate, and stand in awe
before the special relationship between us
and the animals who share our lives.

Pets
part of the family

Dogspeak

Contributing Writers

Susan Easterly, Elaine Waldorf Gewirtz, Bette LaGow,
Susan McCullough, Arden Moore, Liz Palika, Audrey Pavia

Rodale Books

Editor: Matthew Hoffman
Publisher: Neil Wertheimer
Editorial Director: Michael Ward
Research Manager: Ann Gossy Yermish
Copy Manager: Lisa D. Andruscavage
Cover Designer and Design Coordinator: Joanna Reinhart
Associate Studio Manager: Thomas P. Aczel
Book Manufacturing Director: Helen Clogston
Manufacturing Manager: Mark Krahforst

Weldon Owen Pty Ltd

Chairman: John Owen
Publisher: Sheena Coupe
Associate Publisher: Lynn Humphries
Senior Editor: Janine Flew
Project Editor: Kathy Metcalfe
Copy Editor: Lynn Cole, Laura J. Wallace
Senior Designer: Kylie Mulquin
Designer: Jocelyne Best
Picture Researcher: Jenny Mills
Illustrator: Chris Wilson/Merilake
Icons: Matt Graif, Chris Wilson/Merilake
Indexer: Garry Cousins
Production Manager: Caroline Webber
Production Assistant: Kylie Lawson

Film separation by Colourscan Co. Pte. Ltd., Singapore

CONTENTS

PART FOUR

FAILURE TO COMMUNICATE

PART FIVE

PUTTING IT TO WORK

Introduction

Webster's hasn't come out with *The First International Dogtionary*, and that's a shame. Dogs and people have been living together for thousands of years, but despite that, our communication skills are still pretty rocky. We say "Come!" and our dogs hear "Smell the tree over there!" They politely sniff us by way of introduction, and we get offended at their rudeness. We ask them to sleep on the bed, only to watch them take over the couch. Sometimes it seems as though we're speaking different languages.

Which we are. No matter how intelligent and alert they may be, dogs have ways of hearing, seeing, and thinking about the world that are totally different than ours, and this invariably leads to confusion.

I once met a beautiful Irish setter in a park in New York City. He was tossing a tennis ball in the air with his mouth, scrambling after it, and tossing it again. When he saw me he ran over, dropped the ball on the grass, and stared up at me eagerly, his tail whipping the air behind him. I bent over to pick up the ball—and froze when

I heard an ominous *grrr*. Had this friendly Dr. Jekyll turned into Mr. Hyde? I looked at the dog and he looked back, his tail beating a little more. I reached for the ball again. *Grrr.*

A soggy tennis ball wasn't worth getting nailed for, so I walked away. "That's one confused pooch," I muttered.

When I got home I told the story to an animal behaviorist friend of mine, who immediately set me straight. The dog wasn't confused at all, he explained. I was. The dog's "happy" signals all meant the opposite of what I thought. The staring, the wagging tail, and the alert expression were actually challenges. In a playful sort of way, the dog was daring me to pick up the ball. By misunderstanding "dogspeak," I essentially committed a canine faux pas.

The editors at *Pets: Part of the Family* decided to unravel this confusion once and for all. After all, one of the hardest parts of living with dogs is that they can't tell us in words what they're feeling or when they're happy or sad. They can't explain why they're chewing shoes, having accidents in the house, or are terrified of thunder. They can't explain why one training technique is working and another isn't. It's up to us to work out what they're trying to say—and to make sure that they understand us, as well.

We talked to dozens of the country's top behaviorists, trainers, and veterinarians, and asked them to explain the complex world of canine communication and to show us how to communicate a little better, whether we're working out the rules of a ball-toss game or having a heartfelt chat about our dogs' lavatory habits.

Dogspeak is their answer. It's a complete "dogtionary" to help you communicate more effectively and affectionately with the dogs in your life. Much to our surprise, we discovered that barking is just one way—and a minor one, at that—in which dogs communicate. To really understand dogs, you have to *look* at what they're saying. Whether the position of their ears indicates that they're happy or sad. The difference between a friendly tail-wag and a warning tail-swish. When eye contact means "I love you" and when it means "Keep away." Even dogs' facial expressions tell a lot about what they're feeling. *Dogspeak* includes more than 170 photos and illustrations so you can see exactly what to look for.

Communication goes both ways, of course, so this book is packed with tips showing how to help your dog understand you. When to raise your voice higher and when to pitch it low. "Strong" words dogs respond to. The best and worst names for dogs (dogs named Mo sometimes get confused because it sounds like "no"). Hand movements they respond to and those that make them nervous. And much more.

Every page of *Dogspeak* provides fascinating glimpses into dogs' inner lives: How they see. What they really hear. Why smell is so important. You'll also learn some amazing ways to use this information to communicate a little more clearly. And that's what good relationships are all about.

Matthew Hoffman

Matthew Hoffman
Editor, *Pets: Part of the Family* books

PART ONE

WHAT'S YOUR DOG SAYING?

Dogs have plenty to say, but they don't say it the same way we do.
Dogs talk to humans and other dogs through body language and facial
expressions, and by barking, whining, growling, and howling.
They also depend on their senses of smell and hearing,
which are far more sensitive than ours.

CHAPTER ONE

TALK TO YOUR DOG

Dogs are an important and well-loved part of the family. You'll be sharing
your life with your dog for a long time, so improving your relationship
through better communication will have long-term benefits for both of you.

D ogs have an uncanny ability to understand what people are feeling. They don't hold grudges. They love us despite our flaws, and they're there for us day after day. Our relationships with dogs can outlast jobs, friendships, and even marriages. So it's hardly surprising that most people talk to their dogs. They really are our best friends.

"Dogs are full-fledged members of families," says Marty Becker, D.V.M., a veterinarian in Bonner's Ferry, Idaho, and co-author of *Chicken Soup for the Pet Lover's Soul.* "Although we don't speak a lick of Labrador, direct communication is going on between us and our dogs all the time. Dogs sense our moods and allow us to be completely ourselves."

It's not only the human members of the family who appreciate the close ties. In addition to the obvious perks—free food, comfortable places to sleep, and regular belly-rubs—dogs get tremendous emotional fulfillment from their relationships with us. They're naturally social and see people as part of their pack—the canine equivalent of a happy home. "Lying around and listening to us talk is part of what being in this human pack is all about," says Mary Merchant, a therapy dog evaluator for St. John's Ambulance Corps in Powassan, Ontario, Canada.

When they lived in the wild, dogs roamed in close-knit groups called packs. For this golden retriever, his human family has become his pack.

Breaking the Barriers

Even though our relationships with dogs have some "human" qualities, such as mutual respect and affection, there's an inevitable distance between us. We belong to different species, after all, and we see the world and communicate in entirely different ways. Sometimes dogs are telling us things we can't understand. And sometimes we want to tell them things but don't know the best ways to express them. This doesn't mean we can't talk to our dogs. It just means we have to try a little harder.

"When people have difficulty relating to dogs, it's usually because they assume that dogs are just like them," says Jeff Nichol, D.V.M., a veterinarian and a newspaper columnist in Albuquerque, New Mexico.

But dogs aren't like people, which is why words and gestures that have such resonance with us mean nothing at all to them—or, in some cases, mean precisely the opposite of what we're trying to say.

Hugging is a good example. Among people, a full-body hug is a wonderful sign of affection. But dogs don't feel that way. The nearest they come to hugging is when one dog, in an attempt to dominate, pins another dog's shoulders with her paws. So dogs may perceive hugs—from humans or other dogs—as signs of competition rather than affection.

While dogs are more likely to misconstrue gestures than words, they don't have a lot of words to choose from. That's why spoken communication can be the hardest barrier to breach.

Not that this stops anyone from trying. People talk to their dogs all the time—about their day at work, whether a new pillow is comfortable, or if it's time to take a walk. Dogs have impeccable manners and always look interested, even though most of the words are probably just a blur of noise. But the words don't matter all that much because, except for their names and a few commands that they understand, dogs mainly respond to intonations and body language. But dogs do understand some words and phrases, as long as they're simple, spoken plainly, and used consistently.

"A long string of words—like 'Sit, sit, sit, I said, sit'—has no meaning," Merchant says. "It just goes over your dog's head."

Perhaps the best way to communicate more clearly is to spend more time paying attention—not just to your dog's barks, but also to her gestures and body language.

"It takes a lot of practice to be a good listener because we often have preconceived notions of what our dogs are saying," says Laurel Davis,

POOCH PUZZLER

Why don't dogs watch television?

You would think that *The Incredible Journey* or *Lassie* reruns would get any dog's attention, but most dogs don't show a lot of interest in television, regardless of what's on. This is partly because their eyesight isn't very sharp. They're more likely to respond to television sounds, such as barking or phones ringing, than to television images, which probably appear pretty blurry to them.

In the future, however, dogs may spend a lot more time in front of the tube. Big-screen televisions and the development of digital signals have made televised images incredibly lifelike. "With these TVs the pixels are extremely dense, giving an image and sound like never before," says John C. Wright, Ph.D., a certified applied animal behaviorist and professor of psychology at Mercer University in Macon, Georgia. "Your dog may perceive the dog on TV as being real."

POOCH PUZZLER

Are some dogs multilingual?

German, Italian, Swahili—whatever the language, most dogs can understand it, if only because they comprehend the body cues and tone of voice that go with the words.

Some languages, however, are more effective than others for getting a dog's attention. The hard-edged, gruff sound of German has more of a "commanding" ring to it than the lyrical, lighter tones of French, for example. A dog who's given a command in German may not have a clue what the word means, but it'll sound important enough to warrant a check of the speaker's body language to see what's expected.

Misty, a Border collie mix, was multilingual. She could react to commands given in Latin, French, Spanish, and English, says Joanne Howl, D.V.M., a veterinarian in private practice in West River, Maryland. Dr. Howl would look at Misty, lift her index finger and thumb, say "Bang, you're dead," or "Tu es morte" and Misty would fall over, stick her legs in the air, and dramatically "die" on cue.

Dogs also seem to be multilingual when it comes to reading the body language of different breeds.

"When dogs approach another dog with their tails pointed straight up, it's viewed as a threat," says John C. Wright, Ph.D., a certified animal behaviorist and professor of psychology at Mercer University in Macon, Georgia. "But a German shepherd somehow knows that a beagle always walks with his tail up. The German shepherd can discriminate the difference in meaning."

D.V.M., a veterinarian in private practice in Asheville, North Carolina. "If you take the time to listen, you can learn a lot from your dog."

Seeing the World Their Way

Dogs are perfectly at home in the human family, but conflicts are nearly inevitable because dogs and people live by different rules and can see similar situations in entirely different ways. For example, you get excited when the mail arrives, but your dog hears an intruder; she looks lazy when she won't move away from the door, but she's probably issuing a challenge; you buy her an expensive dog bed, but she keeps climbing into the armchair—not, it turns out, because it's softer, but because it's higher, and that makes her feel more powerful.

Talking with dogs involves much more than giving commands. It requires understanding why they do the things they do. The most important thing to remember is that dogs originally lived in cohesive, highly structured societies called packs. Nearly everything your dog does, from rolling over on her back to grumbling when you tell her to get off the couch, is motivated by her desire to establish her place in the family "pack."

That's not to say that every dog wants to be the boss; in fact, most prefer not to be. But they derive tremendous comfort from knowing what their status is in the family, says John Loomis, owner of Alibi Obedience and Agility Training School in Jacksonville, Arkansas. That's why one of the main rules in human relationships—the rule that everyone is created equal—never works with dogs.

"It's not what you say but how you say it that counts," explains Janice DeMello, a trainer in Somis, California. When you're telling your dog to get off the furniture, don't make it sound like a request. Requests work with people but rarely with dogs. When giving commands, make them sound like commands—firm and authoritative. Your dog will understand that you mean business, and, more important, she'll be reminded that her status in the family is lower than yours. Rather than resenting this, she'll be able to relax because she'll know exactly where she stands.

Talking with dogs isn't just about telling them to do things. It's about understanding what they're feeling at any particular time. Dogs aren't very verbal, but their body language, facial expressions, and movements provide tremendous insights into what they're thinking and feeling. "You can learn a lot about your dog just by watching her," says Amy Ammen, director of Amiable Dog Training in

Communicating effectively with dogs isn't just about giving clear verbal messages, you also need to understand their motivations for doing things.

Milwaukee and author of *Training in No Time.* When you watch dogs closely, you'll learn to recognize more than the obvious emotions like happiness or sadness. You'll know when they're feeling restless or bored, when they want attention, and even what they're about to do next.

Dogs are as complex as people, and they often give conflicting signals. The tail may be saying "Play with me!" while the eyes are saying "I'm feeling pretty tense right now." This is why you can't follow the same rules when dealing with all dogs. But once you're familiar with your dog's usual habits and expressions, you'll know exactly what she's feeling—and, most of the time, what she's trying to tell you. You'll develop a strong sense of empathy, and that's what friendship is all about.

BREED SPECIFIC

German shepherds are among the most popular service dogs because they're very skilled at understanding what people want them to do. This has less to do with native intelligence than with their instinctive urge to please their owners. More than most breeds, German shepherds are attuned to the people they spend time with, which makes it easy for them to learn spoken commands, hand signals, facial expressions, and body language.

CHAPTER TWO

How Dogs Talk with Dogs

Dogs are expert communicators, using not only their voices, but also body language, facial expressions, and scent. Other dogs get the messages far more quickly than we do, but if you watch closely, you'll soon learn what they are saying to each other.

Dogs don't waste much time getting acquainted. Within seconds of meeting, they've worked out one another's sex, age, and status, and come to a tacit understanding as to which dog has the higher status. At that point they'll either begin to play or go their separate ways. Or, if there is some dispute about who is top dog, they may settle the argument with a brief, but rarely serious, tussle.

It seems amazing that dogs can collect so much information so quickly, but it's really not surprising. Like people, dogs rely on more than just their voices to communicate. They use everything from body language and scent to facial expressions to say their piece.

What Dogs Have to Say

Dogs have plenty to say, and much of it harkens back to their past. Because they're pack animals, they spend time sorting out their status—who fits where in the social structure, and who gives the orders. They also talk about establishing and defending their territory and possessions, such as food, toys, or even (in their view) humans.

"Although their emotions don't linger like ours, dogs also feel fear, excitement, happiness, stress, uncertainty, and confusion," says Chris Kemper, a dog trainer in Dallas, Texas. And, unlike people, dogs have no reason to camouflage their emotions. Simply watching how they act and react when they're together will give you a good idea of what they're trying to say.

Both these dogs are communicating many things with their body language. The keeshond (left) is interested in his new friend, but is maintaining dominance by standing stiff and tall. The Welsh springer spaniel's pose is friendly, but definitely submissive.

Learning to Communicate

During the first seven or eight weeks of life, puppies learn the basics of communication from the best teacher of all—their mother. For instance, when she wants to start weaning them (about the time those sharp little puppy teeth come in), she'll curl her lip at them. This warns them to back off, says Wendy Volhard, a trainer in Phoenix, New York. "If they persist, she'll growl a little. If she still hasn't gotten through, she'll really growl, which lets them know she means business," she says.

Conversely, the mother lets them know what's acceptable by ignoring or casually accepting their actions. "If one pup is grabbing another's ears just in play, not to hurt him, his mother lets him know, by ignoring his behavior, that what he's doing is fine," says Marge Gibbs, a trainer in Lincolnshire, Illinois, and a columnist for *The American Kennel Club Gazette*.

Puppies quickly learn to talk to each other, too. Because they play by biting, an important message is, "Hey, that hurts." When one puppy bites a littermate too hard, the victim squeals, letting the biter know he went too far. Puppies soon learn to "inhibit" their bites, which ensures they'll all get along. "You can yelp like a puppy to stop them from biting you," says Volhard. "It's far more effective than any verbal command because you're speaking their language."

Talking with Body Language

Throughout a dog's life, body language will remain his most important way of talking to other dogs. He'll use his eyes, tail, ears, and general

POOCH PUZZLER

Why do dogs form barking chains?

If you live in a neighborhood with more than one dog, you will have heard the infamous "barking chain," the canine equivalent of a musical round. One dog starts the din, and soon others in nearby yards join in.

Sometimes they're all barking at the same thing, such as when a bicyclist passes each house. But at other times, it's anybody's guess what got that first dog started.

"With group activities, sometimes it's a matter of trying to look—or in this case, sound—bigger than you are," says Mark Feinstein, Ph.D., an animal behaviorist and dean of cognitive sciences at Hampshire College in Amherst, Massachusetts. "You see this with clustering behavior in cattle, and perhaps the barking chain is a similar thing."

Some dogs, however, are less likely to join in. Large working breeds, such as Kuvaszok or Maremma sheepdogs, would be among the first to bow out of the barking chain because they've been bred to live among their charges, and making too much noise would upset the herds. But scent hounds such as bassets and bloodhounds are very vocal, as are terriers, whose traditional role was to bark to let their owners know they'd found game or vermin.

stance to let them know what's on his mind. When two dogs meet, the first thing they do is establish their rank. A dog who wants to say, "I'm confident, I'm fearless, and what are you going to do about it?" does so by putting his head, tail, ears, and hackles up and by making eye contact. If another dog of lesser rank wants

These Rhodesian ridgebacks are having a great time play-fighting. The lower-ranking dog is submitting by rolling over with his belly up.

to reply, "Not a thing, boss," he'll lower his tail and ears and possibly crouch or lick his lips.

When a dog wants to invite another dog to play, there's no mistaking his message. "He's happy, panting, grinning, and his tail is wagging so hard that his whole rear end is wiggling," says Gibbs. He may drop into a play-bow, then back up and pretend to run—anything to entice his friend to a quick game of tag or roughhousing.

On the other hand, if they've been playing hard and one dog decides he's had enough, he'll start ignoring the other dog. If that doesn't work, he might raise a lip, growl, or even snap to get the other dog to back off.

Dogs don't stay angry very long, and one of the dogs will usually try to bring things to a friendly level again. He'll do this by using many of the same gestures he used as a puppy when he wanted some care and consideration. "He will lick the other dog's mouth, roll over, and expose his belly," says Kemper. Or he might use other appeasing gestures, such as flattening his ears, lowering his body and squinting. It's his way of saying, "Treat me nicely, please."

The Role of Play-Fighting

As well as being fun, play-fighting is one way dogs sort out the pecking order. It's also a great way for a lower-ranking dog to challenge, even briefly, another dog whose position he'd never seriously consider usurping. "Often two dogs will stage a mock fight—no blood, just lots of snarls and tussling," says Kemper. "You'll see one laying his head over the shoulders of the other, showing his dominance. In the end, the lower-ranking dog will usually roll over onto his back, which is his way of saying 'uncle.'"

Going belly up is a classic sign of submission from puppyhood, when a pup learned he'd be safe if he rolled over and let the other guy win. A dog won't hurt another who has given in.

Most play-fighting, even at its most genial, has its roots in dominance displays. And some breeds take things a bit more seriously than others, says Gibbs. "Labradors love to play rough, but put some of the herding or Nordic breeds such as malamutes or huskies into the mix and it may become a fight."

Communicating with Scent

For dogs, there's a whole realm of scent-based communication that humans can't even begin to imagine. Dogs can detect and identify

A Body Language Primer

A dog like this vizsla (below) can tell a lot about another dog just by looking at him and noting what the different parts of his body are doing.

Eyes
- Direct eye contact means a dog is feeling bold and confident
- Casual eye contact means he's contented
- An averted gaze means deference
- Dilated pupils indicate fear

Ears
- Relaxed ears mean that a dog is calm
- Erect ears show that a dog is alert and attentive
- Ears that are up and forward mean a dog is challenging or being assertive
- Ears that are laid back indicate that a dog is worried or scared

Body movements
- Pawing is an appeasing gesture
- Licking another dog's face is an invitation to play or a sign of deference
- Play-bowing (front legs extended, rump up, tail wagging) is an invitation to play and a sign of happiness
- Draping the head over another dog's shoulders is a sign of boldness
- Freezing in place means a dog is frightened
- Rubbing or leaning against another dog is a companionable gesture

Mouth and lips
- Panting means that a dog is feeling playful or excited, or maybe he's just hot
- A dog with the mouth and lips closed is uncertain or appeasing
- Licking the lips is a sign a dog is worried or is being appeasing
- A relaxed mouth means a dog is calm
- Lips pulled back are a challenging or warning sign

Hackles (the hair on the shoulders and hips)
- Raised hackles indicate arousal, either because a dog is frightened or is challenging another dog
- Smooth hackles show a dog is calm

Tail
- A relaxed tail means a dog is calm and at ease
- Tail held straight out, wagging rhythmically and slowly, means that a dog is cautious or on guard
- Tail down indicates worry or uncertainty
- Tail held up and wagging fast indicates excitement
- An erect tail is a sign of alertnesss
- A tail between the legs is a sign of fear

smells that humans don't even know exist because dogs' olfactory glands are literally a million times more sensitive to some smells than ours are.

Though we may turn up our noses at the most typical dog greeting—the nose-to-rear-end method—it works well for them. The anal sacs just under a dog's tail contain glandular secretions that vary in composition from dog to dog. Dogs can tell with one sniff more than we'd ever get from a phone call: The other dog's age, sex, rank, health, and whether he or she has been altered.

Dogs pick up and deliver scent messages everywhere they go. One of the main ways they communicate with other dogs is with urine marking. The smell of regular urine differs from the urine that's used for marking. By leaving their mark in various places, dogs let other dogs know that they're claiming possession of this territory. Male dogs are much more inclined to this behavior than female dogs. They're telling any potential intruder, "Enter at your own risk." Even if your dog would actually welcome the company, this behavior is ingrained.

Sniffers can determine the "attitude" of the dog that previously marked. "I once saw a very dominant male dog mark a tree," Kemper says. "Later, a more submissive dog smelled the spot and immediately backed up—he seemed to have a submissive reaction to the urine itself."

Some stud dogs in the show ring have been known to mark their handlers' legs, says Mary Merchant, a collie breeder and therapy dog evaluator for St. John's Ambulance Corps in Powassan, Ontario, Canada. That's because, when faced with so much competition, they feel

Scent-marking is one of the main ways dogs like this Labrador communicate, which is why even a short walk can be interrupted with a dozen toilet breaks.

driven to stake their claim to what is rightfully theirs—in this case, their owners.

On a walk, you'll likely see your dog sniff and urinate at the same places. "He probably smells another dog, thinks, 'Oh, no, that's my tree, not yours,' then re-marks the tree," explains Kemper.

Urine is not the only thing that leaves interesting messages for other dogs to find. Just try pulling a dog away from a pile of another dog's stools. This encounter is just about as good as meeting the other dog in person, since when they do meet, it's the rear end that initially gets the most attention.

When your dog makes a deposit while on a walk, or even in your yard, he may immediately scratch and kick at the ground, perhaps even tossing the stools around. Experts think this is yet another way a dog marks his territory, by spreading his scent as far as possible.

Talking with Voice

Humans are verbal creatures, so it's natural for us to expect that barking is the main way that dogs communicate with each other. To a dog, though, barking is far less important than other forms of communication, such as body language or scent marking.

Still, barks, whines, howls, and growls have a place in the dog dictionary. How your dog "talks" depends on his mood and what he wants. To tell what your dog is really saying, you need to look at a sound in context.

Barking

Barking is the dog equivalent of human conversation. It's a great way to get the attention of a human or another dog. It also announces a dog's territory, and helps relieve stress. Different barks mean different things:

- A series of high-pitched barks means your dog's worried or lonesome and wants attention.
- A single bark in his regular voice means he's curious and alert and is making contact.
- Quick, repetitive, high-pitched barks mean your dog's feeling playful, or has spotted something he wants to chase.
- A low, repetitive bark—the sort your dog makes when a stranger approaches—means he's feeling defensive or protective.

Growling

Growling is an unmistakable warning sign. Dogs use it to tell other dogs or humans to back off. They also growl when they're frightened.

- When your dog combines a growl with a dominance posture, he's feeling aggressive.

- When he combines a growl with a submissive posture, he's feeling fearful or defensive.
- A growl during play isn't aggressive.

Howling

Howling is a dog's equivalent of using the phone—it's how he gets in touch with other dogs, even when they're miles away.

- A sing-song howl is used to contact other dogs, and means your dog is curious or happy.
- Plaintive, mournful howls signal distress.

Whining or Whimpering

Whining and whimpering hark back to puppyhood, when these sounds got him attention.

- When your dog is excited or lonesome, he'll whine or whimper to get your attention. These can sound like yawns.
- When he's stressed, fearful, or worried, he'll give repetitive, squeaky whines that may be punctuated with shrill yaps.

BREED SPECIFIC

Some dogs unwittingly challenge others because their ears and tails are naturally in an "aggressive" position. Breeds with pricked ears and tails over their backs, like Akitas, basenjis, and Alaskan malamutes, may get extra attention from dominant dogs because they look ready to fight, even when aggression isn't on their minds. Pups who've recently had their ears cropped, such as Great Danes, Doberman pinschers, and boxers, can also unintentionally set off warning bells in other dogs.

CHAPTER THREE

How Dogs Talk with People

When dogs want to talk with people, they do more than just bark.
They use an eloquent range of body language to say what
they're thinking and tell you what they want.

A dog looks longingly at his leash and paces back and forth in front of the door. The message is obvious: "Hey, I want to go outside." Another dog stands stiffly, his ears up and his tail sweeping slowly back and forth. His body language and his low, throaty growl are saying, "I don't like this situation and you'd better watch out."

Yet another does a full-body dance, barks, and wets the floor whenever his owner comes home. His message is, "You're number one in my book, and I'm peeing just to show that I know you're in charge."

Then there's Sir Loin, a people-pleasing black Labrador who lives with Marty and Teresa Becker in Bonner's Ferry, Idaho. Sir Loin adores having his belly rubbed, and his usual con is to step in front of the Beckers, collapse in an exaggerated fall, and roll onto his back, with his belly exposed and his tail wagging at turbo speed.

"If we're rushing and don't have time to rub his belly, he hangs his head and pouts," says Dr. Becker, a veterinarian and co-author of *Chicken Soup for the Pet Lover's Soul*. "His message is very clear: We've disappointed him."

Each of these dogs is delivering a different message, but they have one thing in common: a rich vocabulary that consists of body language,

Some messages are as obvious as this terrier mix's "Let me in" plea. Others are harder to interpret.

eye contact, behavior, barks, and a variety of other vocal sounds.

Dogs can't master the spoken word, but they don't really need to because they're already experts at getting their owners' attention. Why bother with words when a playful bark, a wagging tail, a cocked head, a lifted paw, or a soulful look in the eyes can deliver such unmistakable messages?

Signals You Should Know

There are slight differences among different breeds, and even among individual dogs, but all dogs communicate in more or less similar ways. People can usually tell what their dogs are feeling by glancing at the ways they're standing or moving, or just by looking at their eyes. But some of their signals aren't that obvious. Here are some of the main ways in which dogs communicate with people—and, in some cases, with other dogs as well.

Barking. There are many reasons dogs bark. It can mean they're having fun or are feeling frightened or lonely. It can mean they want attention or that they hear a strange noise that they think their owners should know about. The tone of barking changes with the dog's motivation, says David S. Spiegel, V.M.D., a veterinarian in private practice in Wilmington, Delaware, who specializes in behavior problems. "A panicked or anxious dog barks in a tone and pattern that we recognize as distress. This is meant to draw us near to help him."

While most dogs bark to say something, others do it just for fun, or out of habit, or because they're bored. This kind of barking can go on all day, and your dog will soon become the neighborhood nuisance.

Chewing. Chewing is natural and dogs get a lot of fun and satisfaction from doing it. Except for puppies who haven't yet learned household rules, dogs quickly learn what is and isn't appropriate for them to chew. So it's rarely a mistake when an adult dog rips up a pair of loafers or chews up a magazine, says Suzanne B. Johnson, Ph.D., an animal behaviorist in private practice in Washington, D.C. Chewing usually means they're anxious or bored. It can also mean they have too much energy and aren't getting enough exercise to dispel it.

Leaning. Dogs are enormously tactile and they don't respect "personal space" quite as much as people do. It's very common for dogs to get close to people and lean against their legs. Our usual reaction is to reach down to scratch their heads—which may not be the response they were after at all.

Dogs who merely lean, as opposed to a catlike rubbing back and forth, may be attempting to expand their personal space by taking over yours. It's sometimes the canine equivalent of leaning forward aggressively and saying "I'm tough and I can do as I like."

Conversely, some dogs lean as a way of expressing affection and establishing possession, much as people put their arms around each other when walking down the street. "My dog, Kira, will lean against me to prevent me from going somewhere else," says Joanne Howl, D.V.M., a veterinarian in private practice in West River, Maryland.

And sometimes, of course, a lean just means your dog is a little itchy and is rubbing against your legs to scratch a hard-to-reach spot.

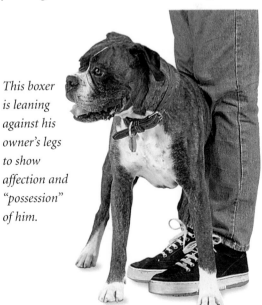

This boxer is leaning against his owner's legs to show affection and "possession" of him.

This young Labrador licks his owner's face in a gesture of deference and affection.

Leg humping. Nearly all dogs at some time in their lives show a little too much interest in people's legs. It's an unpleasant habit that's not only confined to male dogs. Most dogs either outgrow it or give it up once they've been neutered. Some dogs, however, do it all the time. It's not about sex, it's about power. Dogs who hump people's legs are saying "I'm higher on the totem pole than you," explains Jeff Nichol, D.V.M, a veterinarian and newspaper columnist in Albuquerque, New Mexico.

Licking. At one time, most experts believed that dogs licked people's faces for the same reason they licked their mothers'—as a way of getting something to eat. Today, a dog lick is generally considered more of a tribute than an attempt to solicit food. A dog who licks your face is reaffirming his subordinate status and saying that he loves and respects you. "He's telling you that you're the most wonderful thing that ever walked this Earth," says Dr. Nichol.

Limping. It's not unheard of for dogs to sprain their legs, but it occurs a lot less often than their theatrical limps might suggest. Many dogs employ this classic "pay attention to me" signal, and even experts can get fooled. One rainy evening in New York City, Robert Eckstein, D.V.M., Ph.D., a specialist in animal behavior at the department of biology at Warren Wilson College in Asheville, North Carolina, fell victim to the acting ability of a pooch pretender.

"I spotted this stray dog walking on three legs as though his fourth leg were injured beyond use. Once inside my apartment, the dog ran at full speed on all four legs and jumped on the bed. Mission accomplished."

Mouthing hands. Dogs who wrap their muzzles around your hand without using their teeth are giving a friendly greeting. This is common in Labradors and other retrieving dogs who have been bred to gently carry game back to their owners, says Laurel Davis, D.V.M., a veterinarian in private practice in Asheville, North Carolina. Muzzle-wraps aren't always gentle, however. When dogs are playing, one will often use his mouth to shut another's muzzle. Dogs who use their teeth, even in a controlled way, on people are getting way too aggressive, and this type of behavior is often followed by other forms of aggression.

Nose-nudging. Dogs love to push people with their noses. Most of the time it just means they want affection, says Dr. Nichol. "Or he considers the chair that you're in to be his favorite place and he wants you to move out of the way so he can take possession," he adds.

Smiling. Chesapeake Bay retrievers are known for curling their upper lips whenever they feel happy. Alaskan malamutes and Samoyeds are also well-known for their smiling expressions. Most dogs, however, don't smile in the same way that people do. If anything, they tend to assume a grinlike expression when they're feeling threatened and aggressive and want people to see their teeth.

Tongue-flicking. Dogs who repeatedly flick their tongues up to lick their noses are invariably uneasy, says Judy Iby, a registered veterinary technician in Milford, Ohio, and author of *The New Owner's Guide to Cocker Spaniels*. They often do this when they're assessing a new situation or debating whether or not to approach a stranger, she says. It's also common for them to flick their tongues when they're concentrating extra hard, such as during an obedience session.

Yawning. People usually yawn when they're tired or bored, but among dogs, yawning is often a signal that they're feeling stressed. A good yawn briefly lowers their blood pressure and helps them stay calm, says Dr. Howl. She once treated a frightened collie mix, who crouched and shivered on the floor. After Dr. Howl stroked her head and body for a few minutes and spoke some soothing words, the dog let out a huge yawn and stood up.

"After three or four more good yawns, she had calmed down and become my best buddy," says Dr. Howl. "It was fascinating to watch the anxiety pour out of her body."

Lost in Translation

People and dogs speak different languages, so it's not uncommon to misinterpret the messages being passed back and forth. Sometimes we don't understand what our dogs are telling us. More often, they attempt to tell us things, but we don't even recognize that what we're seeing or hearing is a message.

Suppose your dog has started digging holes in the backyard and nothing you do will make him stop. This is more than a behavior problem: It's probably your dog's way of saying that he's a little bored with the daily routine and lack of mental stimulation, and he's trying to shake things up. Knowing the motivation for your dog's behavior is the key to changing it—or, when it's good behavior, encouraging more of it.

When dogs feel a little stressed, they'll often yawn to calm themselves down.

Puppy Surprise

It was late November and a winter storm was coming in—not the best time to deliver a litter of puppies. But dogs can't ignore the call of Nature any more than people can, so that's precisely when a Great Pyrenees named Seminole disappeared from Beverly Coate's farm in Stigler, Oklahoma.

For three days, Beverly looked for Seminole and her new pups. Temperatures were dropping, the wind was picking up strength, and rain was turning to freezing sleet. "I kept thinking about her and telling her in my mind to come and get me," Beverly says. Maybe it was a coincidence, but her positive thinking paid off. At 8:00 P.M., a weather-worn but insistent Seminole showed up in the barn—without her pups.

Seminole ran right to Beverly. She barked and pawed and did everything she could think of to get her attention. "She seemed very agitated with me for taking too long to find the flashlight," Beverly says. "Even though she looked hungry and thirsty, she refused food or water. She just wanted to go."

The two headed into the nearby woods. Sometimes Seminole walked at Beverly's heels, and sometimes she gave her a tug as though providing directions. About a quarter-mile away, Seminole led Beverly to a cedar thicket—and to her litter of nine beautiful pups.

Because dogs are companion animals, it's natural for them to prefer being with their owners than off by themselves. Many of the signals dogs give, from tail-wags to chewing on table legs, are really bids for attention. A dog who grabs his owner's wallet and starts running around the house isn't trying to get change for a twenty. He does it because he knows his owner is going to chase him. When that happens, he'll have succeeded in getting someone to play, and that's what he was after all along.

Every dog acts up (and acts out) occasionally, and it doesn't mean that terrible psychological forces are at work. The messages that dogs try to send are often quite simple: "I'm lonely," or "I'm jealous," or "I'm bored." They don't misbehave because they're trying to get even or cause problems. And they don't misbehave deliberately to tell you what's bothering them. "These acts are not usually deliberate communications with their owners," says Dr. Howl. "They are expressions of what's going on in the dog's mind."

When translating dogspeak, it's helpful to consider your dog's breed, says Steve Aiken, an animal behaviorist in Wichita, Kansas. You can't ignore a dog's inherent tendencies because they're sure to come out one way or another.

"Because terriers were bred to dig out and kill underground rodents, it's natural that they will want to go excavating in your backyard," Aiken says.

You don't have to like that instinct—any more than you have to appreciate a Labrador's instinct to chew—but you can work with it, Aiken says. Some people provide their dogs with authorized digging areas, places where they can excavate to their heart's content. and nearly everyone gives their dogs nice things to chew. By understanding what dogs need, Aiken says, you can give them what they need before they have to ask.

CHAPTER FOUR

CAN YOUR DOG READ YOUR MIND?

Some dogs seem to have extraordinary powers. They can find their way
home over great distances and can even predict earthquakes.
Some people are convinced that dogs can read minds, as well.

They rouse themselves from naps and wander to the door minutes before their owners pull into the driveway—long before they could have heard the sound of an engine or the tires on the road. Dogs who usually love car trips will run away when it's time to go for their annual shots. Some dogs can sense when their owners are going to have a seizure, and others can detect early-stage skin cancer—in some cases, with 99 percent accuracy. To the

human mind, these and other forms of "mind-reading" are nothing less than astonishing, but for dogs, they're all in a day's work.

"I've been a pet lover all my life and a veterinarian for more than 20 years, but I still can't explain how lost dogs find their way back home or act as healers when we're sick or in need," says Marty Becker, D.V.M., a veterinarian in Bonner's Ferry, Idaho, and co-author of *Chicken Soup for the Pet Lover's Soul*. "I don't know if they read our minds or our hearts, but they constantly amaze me by what they pick up."

Mind Over Car

People have been speculating about dogs' extrasensory powers for centuries. Most experts have dismissed stories about canine prescience as being coincidence, at best, or even outright fraud. But one scientist isn't so sure. Rupert Sheldrake, Ph.D., former director of studies in biochemistry and cell biology at Cambridge

*No one's sure how they do it, but but some dogs can
find their way home from hundreds of miles away.*

University, England, and author of *Seven Experiments That Could Change the World*, describes an experiment conducted by an Australian television crew. Having heard that a mixed-breed dog named JT could accurately predict the return of his owner to her home in Manchester, England, they decided to check it out. They designed an experiment in which JT and his owner were recorded simultaneously, with the images being projected on a split-screen television. The test showed convincingly that whenever JT's far-away owner headed for her car to go home, JT would move to the French doors of his home and settle down to greet her. The return trips were entirely random, yet JT got his timing right 85 percent of the time.

"I've collected a database of more than 2,000 pet stories, and there seems to be no clear dominance by breed or intelligence levels," explains Dr. Sheldrake. "The key behind telepathic pet phenomena seems to be the degree of bonding between the pet and his owner."

In the Realm of the Senses

No one can say for sure whether dogs can predict the future or read their owners' minds. But experts agree that dogs and many other animals have senses that go beyond what we can easily imagine, which may explain their uncanny ability to travel great distances without benefit of a compass or map. Homing pigeons use both the configurations of the stars and the Earth's magnetic fields to find their way home. Flocks of monarch butterflies spend their winters in Mexico, then fly back to the Rocky Mountains in Colorado. And there are many verified stories

POOCH ?? PUZZLER

Can dogs predict earthquakes?

Scientists aren't sure how they do it, but some dogs are able to predict earthquakes long before the first tremor shakes the ground. Along with high-tech scientific instruments, dogs (and other animals) are considered an essential part of national earthquake warning systems in Japan and China. Experts have found that hours or even days before earthquakes, dogs begin pacing and acting restless. They bark at nothing and, in some cases, run away from the area.

In 1975, officials in the Chinese city of Haicheng were sufficiently alarmed by unusual animal behavior that they ordered 90,000 residents to evacuate the city. Hours later, a massive earthquake struck. It measured 7.3 on the Richter scale and destroyed 90 percent of the city's buildings. Without the early canine warning, the human tragedy would have been much more severe.

Researchers around the world, including members of the United States Geological Society, have studied how dogs seem to know about earthquakes. They speculate that dogs may detect high-frequency noises deep inside the Earth—noises that are too high for humans to hear. It's also possible that dogs sense electrostatic charges in the atmosphere or vibrations in the Earth. "Dogs have much more acute senses of hearing and smell than we do," says Robert Eckstein, D.V.M., Ph.D., an animal behaviorist in the department of biology at Warren Wilson College in Asheville, North Carolina. "They sense aspects of the real world that we aren't aware of."

of dogs finding their way home after moving to new cities hundreds of miles away.

Even though JT's story suggests that dogs are able to communicate over great distances with their owners, researchers suspect that the explanation has less to do with telepathy than with their incredible senses.

Seizure dogs are a good example. Increasingly used as an "early-warning system" by people who have epilepsy, these dogs have the amazing capacity to warn their owners of oncoming seizures as much as an hour before they occur. This advance notice allows their owners to take precautions, such as sitting down or moving away from stairs, so that they don't injure themselves when the seizure strikes.

The ability to detect seizures sounds as though it could only happen in a high-tech laboratory—or in a late-night science fiction movie. But there's a perfectly plausible explanation, says Roger Reep, associate professor at the University of Florida College of Veterinary Medicine in Gainesville. It's possible, he explains, that dogs are able to predict seizures because their highly developed sense of smell allows them to detect chemical changes in the brain that precede attacks.

In fact, many stories of canine "telepathy" are probably due to dogs' superior senses as well as their superlative observational skills, says Robert Eckstein, D.V.M., Ph.D., an animal behaviorist in the department of biology at Warren Wilson College in Asheville, North Carolina. "Since dogs mainly communicate nonverbally, it's very likely that they read our bodies, not our minds," Dr. Eckstein says. This may explain why your dog suddenly jumps up and looks at you expectantly just when you're thinking of taking him for walk or filling his food bowl. People are always giving off unconscious signals. Your dog probably reads the various movements of your body—the way you glance at the cupboard door or shift your weight, or even changes in your breathing. Some body language is so subtle that another person would never notice it. But dogs notice because at one time their survival depended on their powers of observation. When they lived in tight-knit groups called packs, each dog needed to know how the other dogs were feeling or what they were about to do. Dogs learned that being observant gave them an advantage in the struggle to survive, and they still haven't lost touch with their ancient heritage.

Mental Connections

While most scientists doubt that dogs can read minds, some vets believe that dogs do it every day—and that it's possible for humans to read their pets' minds, too. Laurel Davis, D.V.M., a veterinarian in private practice in Asheville, North Carolina, incorporates in her practice both mainstream veterinary medicine and occasional forays into telepathy. She believes that people have a natural ability to communicate telepathically, an ability that's often strongest in children and tends to become rusty in adults.

Even people who have never given a thought to telepathy have the ability to communicate with their pets, says Dr. Davis. She tells the story of a woman who had just attended an animal communication seminar. After it was over, she saw a man and a big dog sitting in a parked car.

MIND TO MIND

Communicating across the species isn't just the stuff of science fiction. When you're ready to try a little telepathy yourself, here's what professional animal communicators advise.

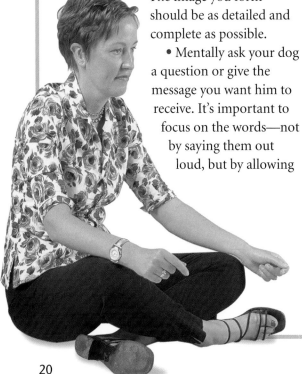

• Set aside a few minutes when you can give your dog your full attention, preferably in a quiet area where you won't be disturbed. Prepare a few questions or messages you want to communicate.

• Take a few deep, relaxing breaths to focus your energy and clear your mind of distractions.

• Say your dog's name in your mind. At the same time, form a detailed mental picture of what he looks like. The image you form should be as detailed and complete as possible.

• Mentally ask your dog a question or give the message you want him to receive. It's important to focus on the words—not by saying them out loud, but by allowing them to form in your mind.

• Relax totally and be prepared for whatever message you receive. In some cases you may hear actual words. More often, you're likely to receive a mental picture or feeling. You may receive a strong feeling that your dog is happy and content. Or you may get a mental image of what he's doing when you're gone or why he's been acting in an unusual way lately. Whatever message you receive, you need to acknowledge it mentally so that your dog knows you received it.

Don't be surprised if you don't receive any mental images at all, adds Laurel Davis, D.V.M., a veterinarian in private practice in Asheville, North Carolina. Most people aren't accustomed to using their minds to communicate with their dogs, and it takes time and practice to learn how to "listen" closely. But it's worth trying. "By talking with dogs on a telepathic level, I've found them to be wiser than you'll ever know," says Dr. Davis. "They are very spiritual."

She decided to try some of the things she had learned at the workshop. She stood still in the parking lot and for 10 minutes spoke mentally with the dog. Then she walked over to the car to say "Hi." The dog greeted her warmly, to the amazement of the owner, who said that his dog had a history of extreme aggressiveness and had never before let anyone near the car.

Patty Summers of Evington, Virginia, is a professional animal communicator. She believes that thought exchange between people and their pets isn't based on the physical senses but on true telepathic communication.

"Because telepathic communication is beyond verbal and isn't physical, it can be done from a distance," she says. "Animals often tune in to their people. They want to know where they are and what they're doing. When someone's coming home, he's probably thinking of heading home. His animal picks up on that thought."

Dr. Davis says she has used her mind to "talk" with dogs who were miles away. She begins these conversations with an ice-breaker, such as asking about their likes and dislikes. (She often finds they really love a particular ball or hate dry dog food.) Once she has established a rapport, she asks them specific questions to help resolve specific problems.

"When I communicate this way with animals, I have to be careful not to let preconceived notions of what I think they're saying or doing enter into the picture," she says. "It takes a lot of practice to be a good listener to dogs."

Mental telepathy takes practice, says Dr. Davis. Even if you aren't able to pick up signals from your dog right away, you can be pretty sure that your dog will hear you—not the actual words, perhaps, but the warmth and positive feelings you're putting out.

Psychic Sasha

Damon Miller couldn't figure out how she did it. On mornings when he planned to stay home from work, Sasha, his white German shepherd, almost went berserk with pleasure. On regular work mornings, she was quiet and almost seemed dejected. The amazing thing was that Sasha seemed to know his plans even before he got dressed in the morning.

Damon and his wife, Kathie, wondered if something was tipping her off. Damon, a dentist in Merlin, Oregon, didn't have a fixed schedule. Sometimes he took Wednesdays off. Occasionally he worked weekends. He rarely announced beforehand when he was going to stay home. But Sasha always knew. She seemed to be reading his mind.

Or maybe she was reading his socks. Damon and Kathie finally realized that Sasha started getting excited—or dejected—as soon as Damon took his socks from the bureau drawer. Brown socks, which he always wore to work, meant he was leaving the house. White socks meant it was going to be a fun, let's-play kind of day. "When Sasha spotted white socks being removed from the drawer, she would jump up and down and act excited," says Kathie. "Damon would pat Sasha's head to confirm that this was 'white socks day,' and they'd head out to his wood shop in the garage and spend the day together."

Was Sasha reading their minds or reading the clues? The Millers still don't know for sure. "We just know that she hated being left at home," Kathie says.

CHAPTER FIVE

THE NOSE KNOWS

One of the main ways that dogs communicate is with their sense of smell.
They sniff other dogs to learn about their age, sex, and status. They can even tell
a lot about a person's mood by the way he smells.

There's a powerful instrument that can detect tobacco wrapped in 27 layers of polythene or locate termites that are silently demolishing the foundations of a house. This instrument isn't a technological marvel created by humans, and you don't need an advanced degree to use it. It's the canine nose.

Among humans, the most important senses are sight and hearing. Among dogs, the sense of smell is paramount. A dog's sense of smell is up to a million times more sensitive than a human's.

Dogs can detect scents we don't even know exist, and they can identify the faintest of smells, even when they're heavily masked by other scents—such as the odor of trace amounts of heroin that have been hidden in pungent aniseed. A dog's sense of smell is often more powerful than the best scientific instruments, which is why dogs have been used to detect not only drugs but also gas leaks and explosives, and to find people lost in the wilderness or buried in avalanches.

Dogs can smell things humans can't because they have more nasal membrane than we do. We

The canine sense of smell is more sensitive than any machine, which is why Customs officers use dogs to search airline passengers' luggage for narcotics.

have about 65 square inches of nasal membrane, while dogs have about 900 square inches—an area that's greater than that of a dog's whole body, says Bruce Fogle, D.V.M., Ph.D., a veterinarian and author of *The Dog's Mind*. The nasal membrane is packed with olfactory receptors, specialized cells responsible for detecting scents.

A German shepherd typically has about 220 million olfactory receptors, while a human has about 5 million, says Mark Plonsky, Ph.D., a psychologist and dog trainer at the University of Wisconsin in Madison. It's believed that the bigger the dog and the longer his muzzle, the keener his sense of smell. German shepherds, for example, aren't just better at sniffing out scents than humans are, they're better at it than some other breeds. A fox terrier, for instance, has 150 million olfactory receptors, and a dachshund has about 125 million.

Dogs have an additional advantage. Their noses are always wet, as anyone knows who has woken up to the sensation of a cold, wet nose. It's believed that this sheen of moisture acts almost like Velcro, trapping scent molecules as they waft by. Along with the sticky mucus in the nasal passages, this allows dogs to collect and store large numbers of passing molecules.

Scents don't just drift conveniently into their noses. A dog's nostrils act like little antennas. Dogs wiggle them to collect scents and figure out where they're coming from.

When your dog raises his head and sniffs, he's breaking his normal breathing pattern to gather some new information. The air currents are abuzz with news, and he can hardly wait to tap into them and find out what's going on. "He has to actively sniff to pull the scent into the olfactory

Detective Down Under

PUPPY DOG TALES

Rex, a wire fox terrier, lived happily in a suburb of Sydney, Australia, for most of his eight years. But when his owners, Rae and Ted Humphries, started spending more time away from home, they decided it would be best for Rex if he went to live with friends more than 20 miles away. "I didn't like the idea of his being lonely all day without us, and I thought he'd be better off where he'd have more company," Rae says.

Rex, however, had different ideas. He ran away from his new home the day after he arrived. His new owners searched the neighborhood for days, but Rex was nowhere to be found. They had to accept that he wasn't coming back.

Three months later, Rae heard a scratching at the back door one evening. She opened the door and there was Rex. "He was thin and his coat was caked with dirt," she says. "But despite his sorry state, he was so happy to see me."

She couldn't imagine how Rex managed to find his way across railroad tracks, traffic-filled highways, and open land to find his family after all those months. "You hear about dogs having a wonderful sense of smell, and I can only imagine that Rex put his to good use to find us," she says. "After that escapade, we knew he had to stay with us."

Dogs like this pharaoh hound sniff the air to collect scent molecules and locate where smells are coming from.

23

sensors, and when he doesn't, he's effectively turning his nose—or his sense of smell—off," says D. Caroline Coile, Ph.D., a neuroscientist in Ochlocknee, Georgia.

What all this means is that dogs have the ability to take in and identify scents that humans don't even know exist.

The scent molecules gleaned with each sniff are ultimately distilled and transported to various parts of the brain, much of which is devoted to remembering and interpreting them. Dogs have the ability to tap into this scent storage bank throughout their lives.

"Odors have a powerful influence on both the behavior and the physiology of the dog," says Dr. Fogle. "Smell memories last for life and affect almost all canine behavior." Scents tell them where they are, who a dog or person is, and even what state of mind that other creature happens to be in.

of information by reading the scent messages that other dogs have left.

The urine of female dogs in heat, for example, contains different pheromones—scent molecules—than that of dogs who are out of season. The males, of course, are eager for this information.

It's not only urine that contains scent signals, says Ian Dunbar, Ph.D., a veterinarian and author of *Dog Behavior*. The anal glands, stools, and saliva also contain olfactory information that dogs are keen to get hold of.

Even though dogs introduce themselves by sniffing each other's faces, it's the back ends that get the most attention. A quick sniff reveals a lot: how old a dog is, which sex, neutered or intact, relative or stranger. Scents also reveal a dog's confidence and social status, and what his mood happens to be at the moment. Dogs synthesize all of this information and figure

How Dogs Communicate with Scent

A dog who raises his leg on a tree isn't being indelicate. He's essentially pinning a notice on the community bulletin board. The scents in urine are as unique as the fingerprints among humans. Dogs who sniff trees, electric poles, and fire hydrants are gleaning tremendous amounts

By putting his nose to work this Border collie is learning the age, sex, and status of other dogs that have been visiting his neighborhood.

These Picardy shepherds are indulging in the usual sniff routine, which enables them to collect a lot of personal information.

out very quickly what their relationship with another dog is likely to be.

Although dogs do the sniffing routine longer with dogs they don't know, even house mates will sniff each other frequently. Behaviorists aren't sure why dogs continue to sniff even when they know each other intimately. It may simply be the dog equivalent of saying "How are you today?" and catching up on the gossip.

A dog's fascination with smells doesn't stop with sniffing. Even dogs that have lived indoors all their lives appear to have an instinct that tells them to get dirty and roll in smelly things at the first opportunity. "It's camouflage," says Torry Weiser, a dog trainer in San Francisco. "What they're doing is using the scent of another creature to disguise themselves from something they're preying on and to get closer to it." Dogs don't have to think about prey and predators very much anymore, but the urge lives on.

"They seem to be having a great time doing it," Weiser adds. "It's not perfume to us, but it certainly is to them."

What Human Scents Tell Dogs

Your dog knows your scent and has it filed in his memory, along with the smells of all the other people he's been introduced to. Some people your dog will remember with affection, others with fear and loathing—and his "scent memory" will be triggered every time he meets them.

The one smell dogs value most is the smell of their owners. "It's a familiar smell that conveys comfort and safety," says Weiser. That's why experts recommend leaving an article of worn clothing with your dog when you have to leave for any length of time. The piece of clothing has your smell on it, and it gives comfort to him.

And like it or not, your dog can tell a lot about your mood just by your smell. A person's body odor is believed to change depending on his or her mood, and dogs are thought to be able to pick up on this.

Research has also shown that "happy tears" contain different chemicals than "angry tears," and some experts believe dogs can tell the difference—and know right away whether to nuzzle your hand or give you a wide berth until you've calmed down.

Perfume, deodorant, cigarette smoke, and other odors that linger on skin and clothing all combine to make up a person's individual smell. Changing that composite smell "picture" in some way—using a new perfume or none at all, for instance—can confuse a dog and dull his

BREED SPECIFIC

Dogs bred to hunt, track, or retrieve, such as bloodhounds, beagles, Norwegian elkhounds (right), and Labrador retrievers, appear to have the best sense of smell. But any dog's sense of smell can be improved with the proper training.

Norwegian elkhounds have an astonishing sense of smell and can detect game up to three miles away.

ability to recognize someone as quickly as he normally would.

Dogs don't care if you're sweaty or have something pungent on your hands, but there are odors that do turn them off. Among these are citrus smells, such as lemon, lime, and orange, and spicy smells like red pepper. They particularly dislike the smell of citronella, which is why it's often used in spray form to keep dogs away from certain areas.

There are odors that turn dogs on, too, and often they're ones that turn us off. The trash smells like a smorgasbord to our dogs, but if we smell it at all, it's the opposite of delectable.

Sometimes, because of illness or accident, a dog's sense of smell can become impaired. "Dogs with a loss of smell seem to do just fine," says Dr. Coile. They'll tend to rely more heavily on their other senses to give them the essential information they need, she explains. They may start to eat less, though. The smell of their food is important to them, even more than the taste. That's why veterinarians often advise warming food when dogs lose their appetites. Warming food boosts the aroma, which may get them eating again.

NOSES AT WORK

Working dogs use their sense of smell to hold down serious jobs. Among the canine professions that call for a good nose are drug sniffing, explosive detection, and rescue work. Specially trained scent dogs can also locate people trapped in avalanches and under rubble.

In California, a group of beagles is employed by the U. S. Department of Agriculture at airports and postal facilities to detect fruits, plants, and meats that are being illegally transported into the state.

Research has shown that dogs' noses contain infrared receptors that are sensitive to temperature. Combined with their sharp sense of smell, these receptors help dogs to detect humans buried deep in snow.

Dogs can also be trained to track people who have gotten lost in wilderness areas. And they can detect shed human skin cells in places where people have recently been.

CHAPTER SIX

BEYOND HUMAN HEARING

Dogs have astonishingly good hearing, and they pay more attention
to sounds than people do. You can take advantage of their
superior hearing to help them learn more quickly.

Can you hear the squeak of a mouse inside a wall, the ultrasonic beep of a dying smoke alarm battery, or the faint sound of a thunderstorm long before it arrives? Not a chance—but for dogs, these and other faint or high-pitched sounds are as loud and clear as the ringing of a bell.

Their superior hearing dates from when they lived in the wild, and the ability to hear the slightest of sounds could mean the difference between getting a meal and going hungry.

Though the need to listen for a meal is long gone, dogs still rely on their hearing to make better sense of the world around them.

Experts have discovered that dogs can hear sounds from four times farther away than people can. That means that what a person can hear from a hundred yards, a dog can hear from a quarter-mile. Dogs are also able to detect very high frequencies that humans are oblivious to.

Dogs may not be able to see with crystal clarity, but they more than make up for that with their exquisitely sensitive hearing. It lets them know that you're coming home long before you pull into the driveway, and they can tell when you're upset no matter how hard you try to keep your voice steady.

A very effective way to work with dogs, whether you're trying to get their attention or helping them learn new commands, is to take advantage of their hearing. Not only do they hear things we can't, they hear things differently. You can use these differences to help dogs learn more quickly, feel more secure, and understand what you're saying.

This Labrador always knows when his owner is coming home because he can distinguish the sound of her car from any other.

Why Dogs Hear So Well

Before dogs became domesticated, hearing was an essential sense for survival. Their sharp hearing alerted them to danger, let them communicate with other dogs far away, and enabled them to detect even the smallest and most cautious prey. The changes in the brain that occurred over thousands of years still guide dogs today. Experts have found, for example, that while the human brain is largely devoted to such things as learning and memory, much of a dog's brain is devoted to sound, says Katherine A. Houpt, V.M.D., Ph.D., a veterinary behaviorist and professor of physiology at Cornell University in Ithaca, New York.

One of the reasons dogs hear so much better than people do is that their ears are bigger. They're also cup-shaped, which enables them to trap all the available sound waves and funnel them into the eardrum. Another advantage is that their ears are as mobile as antennas. Dogs have 15 different muscles that move the ears up, down, and sideways. And they can move one ear at a time—a talent that eludes most people—which lets them detect and pinpoint sounds coming from any direction.

With all of this anatomical sophistication, dogs can do some amazing things—like hearing when a cat's nosing around their food, even when they're sound asleep three rooms away. They can tell, using hearing alone, whether the

SIREN SONG

The high-pitched wail of a siren can launch even quiet dogs into howling harmonies. Dogs can hear sounds at very high frequencies, and experts once suspected that the wail of sirens hurt their ears, just as fingernails against a chalkboard drive some people crazy.

The problem with this theory is that dogs never seem uncomfortable or unhappy when they're howling at sirens. Quite the opposite, in fact: Many dogs seem to relish it. "There's absolutely no evidence that these sounds hurt their ears," says John C. Wright,

Ph.D., a certified applied animal behaviorist, professor of psychology at Mercer University in Macon, Georgia, and author of *The Dog Who Would Be King*.

The most likely explanation, he says, is that dogs evolved from wolves, and wolves howl to greet their pack-mates and to communicate across distances. Dogs are a long way from wolves, but some of the old instincts remain. It's unlikely that they confuse sirens with the greeting of another dog, but they still respond the way they're supposed to—by howling back.

walk?

woof

Can dogs spell?

Some dogs get so excited when they hear words such as "walk" or "cookie" that their owners develop a kind of code to prevent themselves from going bananas. Rather than saying "walk," for example, they'll spell it out and say "w-a-l-k."

But it usually doesn't take dogs long to learn that w-a-l-k means it's time to run about and bark until someone finally picks up the leash.

Even though dogs can't spell, they're perfectly capable of learning complex sound patterns and linking these sounds with what they mean, says Torry Weiser, a dog trainer in San Francisco. "If you spell a word such as 'walk' each time you get ready to take your dog out, eventually, he'll figure out what it means," Weiser explains.

food that slipped from the cutting board was an uninteresting brussels sprout or a tempting piece of meat. Even when they're running around in the backyard, they'll know you're home the instant your key hits the lock.

Dogs' superior hearing makes their world a very interesting place—and also one that's vastly different from a human's world.

"It's hard to imagine what a dog's world must be like," says D. Caroline Coile, Ph.D., a neuroscientist with a special interest in canine sensory systems in Ochlocknee, Georgia. "What we do know is that they certainly have a much richer auditory life than we do."

Despite their excellent hearing, dogs aren't overwhelmed by the variety or volume of the sounds they hear any more than people are overwhelmed by the range of the things they see. Anything dogs aren't interested in or don't need to know, their brains filter out. That's why they can sleep through a noisy conversation in the next room but will wake up the instant someone says their name. Similarly, when someone fills the laundry tub to wash a sweater, some dogs hide because they think it's bathtime—but they'll ignore the sound of the kitchen sink being filled for doing the dishes. They only tune in to the things that might affect them, says Dr. Houpt.

Some of the things that attract a dog's attention are the same things people wish they could hear but can't—like the sound of someone slipping over a back fence into the yard. This is one situation in which a dog's superior hearing is a real favor to the family. But just like car alarms, sometimes a dog's hearing can be a little too sensitive. Dogs will occasionally erupt in a sudden burst of barking because they hear something that the people in the family can't see or hear, and couldn't care less about.

Being able to hear high frequencies has surprising

This Labrador can hear the sounds of small animals under the snow, so he does what comes naturally—he investigates by digging.

benefits for some dogs. The cry of a bat, for example, is way too high for most creatures, including cattle, to hear. That may explain why cattle in South America often get attacked by vampire bats, but dogs seldom do. It seems that dogs can hear the bats' cries and so can avoid becoming the source of their next meal, says Bruce Fogle, D.V.M., Ph.D., author of *The Dog's Mind.*

It seems that all dogs, no matter what their size or breed, have roughly equal hearing abilities, says Rickye Heffner, Ph.D., professor of psychology at the University of Toledo in Ohio. Small dogs don't hear higher frequencies better than large dogs do, and large dogs are no better at picking up low noises than smalls dog are.

Ear type doesn't have much effect on hearing, either. Floppy-eared dogs and prick-eared dogs have fared about the same in tests,

Gretchen on Guard

No one knows the benefits of canine hearing better than Jessica Maurer of Portland, Maine. If it weren't for the keen ears of Gretchen, her 11-year-old Samoyed, Jessica and a few of her friends might not be here to tell the tale.

Jessica, her roommate, and two neighbors had just sat down at an outdoor table in Jessica's backyard. They were about to eat when Gretchen suddenly stood up and began to growl. Jessica looked over and saw that Gretchen was staring up at the 80-foot sycamore tree that loomed over the table.

That's when they heard a loud popping sound. Realizing the tree was about to fall, they scrambled to get out of the way. Jessica's roommate didn't move quickly enough, and her legs were injured. But everyone else got away in time—thanks to an alert dog with very remarkable hearing.

PUPPY DOG TALES

A dog's ear size and shape don't affect how well he hears. Floppy-eared dogs like the Cavalier King Charles spaniel (right) hear just as well as prick-eared ones like the Belgian shepherd (left).

says Dr. Heffner. Surprisingly, dogs with floppy ears can hear almost as well with their ears in the normal, droopy position as when they're taped up to expose the ear canal.

One thing that is breed-related is the likelihood of a dog being born deaf. This is caused by a genetic disorder that is associated with white and blue merle coat colors. "It can crop up anywhere, but it crops up a lot in Dalmatians," says Dr. Heffner. Other breeds commonly affected include Australian cattle dogs, Australian shepherds, Boston terriers, English setters, and Old English sheepdogs.

But dogs who are deaf learn to compensate in other ways. "Dogs spend 80 to 90 percent of their time communicating without a sound," says Suzanne Clothier, a trainer and co-owner of Flying Dog Press in St. Johnsville, New York. They pay close attention to body language, faces, and eyes to help them understand each other and people. Dogs who are deaf learn to "read" people very well.

A Sound Approach

Since dogs are attuned to and excited by high-pitched sounds—probably because these were the sounds made by their traditional prey—the best way to get their attention is by pitching your voice upward, says Clothier. Speaking in a high voice is perfect during training or when you're calling your dog, she explains. It's also an effective way of letting your dog know when he has pleased you.

Dogs also respond to lower tones, presumably because these sounds resemble the growls or grumbles they hear almost from birth—first from their mother when she wanted to reprimand them, and later from dogs who growled to send the message "Leave me alone" or "Don't touch that, it's mine."

Unlike high tones, which tend to make dogs happy and excited and less likely to obey instruction, low tones make them slightly nervous because they associate these sounds with "top dogs." You can use this to your advantage when dogs aren't doing what you want by speaking in a deeper, growl-like voice. They'll understand that you really mean business and so will be more likely to obey you.

You can also get results by playing with the volume of your voice. Shouting will get a dog's attention, but may be counterproductive because it can also scare or intimidate him. Lower volumes will often work better than a shout. For example, whispers can be very effective once a dog is paying attention. Dogs are intrigued by whispers just as humans are, and they'll do the canine equivalent of leaning closer to hear exactly what you're saying.

POOCH PUZZLER

Do dogs like music?

Many dogs seem to react with pleasure when their owners turn up the stereo. They may lie down peacefully at their owners' feet while mellow New Age or classical music is playing, or prick their ears up at the sound of more strident pop music. Experts suspect it's not the kind of music that gets their attention as much as our reaction to it.

"Our dogs are experts at reading body language," says Steve Aiken, an animal behaviorist in Wichita, Kansas. "When we listen to music we enjoy, our bodies show it. We may sway, dance, or hum, but generally any music that improves our mood will result in body language that our dogs like to see. Our bodies say we're happy, so our dogs are happy."

It *is* possible for dogs to develop musical preferences, Aiken says—but there's a very strong likelihood that they'll form a taste for the same sorts of music that their owners prefer to listen to.

When we listen to music that pleases us, dogs may learn to make a positive association toward that style.

"It's not that they're hanging out to hear the latest Pavarotti recording," Aiken says. "But it's obvious that we enjoy listening to him, and that makes them happy, too."

31

PART TWO

THE BARK SIDE

Dogs depend mainly on scent and body language to
communicate, but they do use their voices—both to talk to each
other and to us. You can tell a lot about what dogs are thinking by the
way they bark. And since barking is their native language, you can
communicate more clearly by occasionally barking back.

CHAPTER SEVEN

THE LANGUAGE OF BARKING

Dogs have different barks to convey different messages. They use some barks to speak with other dogs. Other kinds of barks are meant to get their owners' attention or to show that they are happy and excited. Still other barks indicate that they're nervous or anxious.

A few thousand years ago, barking made a lot more sense than it does today. Even though wild dogs lived together in packs, they often went their separate ways during the day to hunt for food or look for mates. Barking enabled them to communicate across great distances. It served both as a long-distance phone call and a community bulletin board—a way of talking to one dog or the entire pack. And unlike scent and body language, which are dogs' preferred ways of communicating, barking didn't leave a physical trail for predators to follow. So even though wild dogs—and their ancestors, the wolves—didn't bark a lot, it came in handy on occasion.

From an evolutionary point of view, barking isn't a very useful trait any more. For one thing, most dogs live in apartments or houses, so they don't need to communicate across great distances. And since dogs live mainly with humans and not other dogs, barking isn't a great way to communicate. It's like going to Rome and only speaking English: People know you're saying something, but haven't the slightest idea what.

Here's the curious thing. Even though barking is less useful today than it used to be, modern dogs do it a lot more than their ancestors did—not because it's a great way to

When living in the wild, dogs barked to communicate across great distances. These Munsterlanders have all their friends close to home, but the tradition continues.

communicate, but because they're not very mature. Like children, they often bark merely to hear themselves speak.

Perpetual Adolescence

As any parent can attest, adolescence is a noisy time. That's equally true among dogs, who can be real chatterboxes when they're growing up,

Barks and Variations

The basenji (left), a breed that originated in Africa, is a medium-size, handsome dog with a distinctive, tightly curled tail. An unusual shape of the larynx, or voice box, is thought to be responsible for the fact that basenjis don't bark. "But they make every other noise under the sun," says Mary Merchant, a therapy dog evaluator for St. John's Ambulance Corps in Powassan, Ontario, Canada. Their most common noise is halfway between a chortle and a yodel.

Despite their rather odd vocalizations, basenjis are quiet more often than most dogs, probably because they once hunted in packs, and being noisy isn't helpful when you're trying to sneak up on your supper.

Another unusual vocalist is one of the world's most elusive wild dogs, the New Guinea singing dog (right). Found in the mountainous interior of Papua New Guinea, these small, red-and-white dogs have a strange bark that sounds like a rooster's crow. The sound travels tremendous distances and helps the isolated packs stay in touch, says Mark Feinstein,

Ph.D., an animal behaviorist and dean of cognitive sciences at Hampshire College in Amherst, Massachusetts. Even singing dogs that never have any physical contact talk to one another over the valleys.

The dogs are naturally solitary and have been called the night dog or black dog—not because of their coloring, but because they're seldom seen, only heard. There's a small colony of singing dogs at Amherst College. The best way to get them to "sing," says Dr. Feinstein, is to walk out of their sight. They'll start vocalizing right away. "They're trying to make contact," he says.

says Mark Feinstein, Ph.D., an animal behaviorist and dean of cognitive sciences at Hampshire College in Amherst, Massachusetts. In the wild, dogs quickly move through adolescence as they mature and begin taking care of themselves. But in today's world, dogs are always dependent on their owners. In a sense, they never grow up entirely. They continue barking

A Bark Saves a Life

PUPPY DOG TALES

A dog who won't stop barking can be a real nuisance. But Nan Duff, a nurse in Ben Avon, Pennsylvania, owes her life to one dog's determined yaps.

Early one summer morning, Nan's chocolate Labrador, Duncan, began barking—and barking. He barked so loud and so long that Nan's neighbor, Lisa Grillo, wondered what was up. "This barking was very different from the way he usually barked," Lisa recalls. "It was high-pitched, like a yelp."

Lisa phoned Nan to ask what was going on. When she didn't answer, Lisa called the police. Then she went outside and saw Duncan, still barking, in the bedroom window of Nan's home across the street.

The police arrived and broke a window to get into the house. They were greeted by Duncan, who raced upstairs to Nan's bedroom. The officers found Nan unconscious in bed, with Duncan at her side. She was taken to the hospital, where doctors learned that her blood sugar was frighteningly low. Nan, a diabetic, had lapsed into a life-threatening coma.

Nan recovered and was amazed when she learned how Duncan had called for help in the only way he could. For his lifesaving effort, Duncan received the Pennsylvania Veterinary Medical Association's Human–Animal Bond Award, which rewards animals whose heroic deeds best exemplify the close bonds between people and their pets.

It's not a coincidence that dogs started barking a lot more when they were domesticated. Their new owners realized that barking could be a useful trait. It warned them when strangers were approaching, it alerted them to the presence of game, and it let strangers know that this was a dog to be reckoned with. Barking was so useful, in fact, that people deliberately bred those dogs who barked the most, and the "vocal" genes were passed on through the generations.

For most people, of course, barking is more of a nuisance than anything else—but dogs keep doing it. That's partly because we often inadvertently encourage barking. For example, people who are walking their dogs will often touch the top of their dogs' heads and admonish them when they make a noise—cues that dogs often take to mean they're doing a great job and should keep it up. A similar thing occurs when sleep-deprived owners stick their heads out the window and yell at a dog to pipe down. Barking dogs are often seeking a reply—any reply—and if it happens to be a human who answers, that'll do fine.

because their domestication has them stuck in adolescence, says Dr. Feinstein.

"It's young dogs that are almost always the barkiest," adds Deborah Jones, Ph.D., a dog trainer in Akron, Ohio. They rarely stop barking completely, but when they're older and more experienced, they tend to bark less. "Once they get better at reading and sending the more subtle body language clues, they quiet down," says Dr. Jones.

Interpreting Barks

Dogs bark for all sorts of reasons. Apart from greeting other dogs, they bark to ask for attention or to show that they're happy and excited.

Barking helps them blow off steam and relieves stress as well as boredom. Dogs have a number of different barks, which convey entirely different messages. By listening to the pace, pitch, and overall tones, you can get a pretty good idea of what your dog's trying to say.

Strong and Steady

Dogs often respond to strangers approaching or things they hear outside with a series of single barks, or with a quick, repetitive *wooo-wooo-wooo-wooo-wooo*. This type of barking is a warning. It's not meant to tell the intruder to go away, but to let the owners know that something is amiss. "He doesn't want to handle this potential threat all by himself, so he calls for reinforcements," says Dr. Jones.

You can't tell from listening to this type of bark whether the intruder is a human or

When a dog barks at strangers from inside the car, his bark will be strong and steady because he's warning you of possible danger.

Even though dogs no longer need to hunt for food, they still have a strong instinct to chase small animals—or at least to bark at them.

another dog. But your dog's body language will provide additional cues, says Dr. Jones. If a strange dog approaches, for example, your dog will probably do a lot of running forward, then stepping back. "But if the other dog is an old pal, look for play-bows, tail wagging, and happy, upright ears."

Dogs give similar greetings when people they recognize come to visit. Even though the bark is low-pitched and regular, it almost sounds happy—a message that will be reinforced by happy panting and tail wags.

Fast and Furious

Dogs don't have the best vision in the world, and from a distance, a running rabbit probably doesn't appear all that different from a person zipping by on in-line skates. So they respond the way they would to anything that's moving quickly, with a high-pitched, fast bark that says,

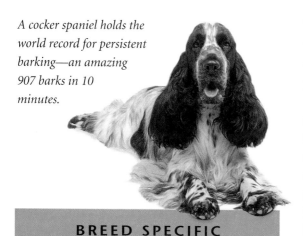

A cocker spaniel holds the world record for persistent barking—an amazing 907 barks in 10 minutes.

BREED SPECIFIC

Nearly all dogs bark occasionally, but some breeds have a stronger tendency to bark than others. This is because they were bred to use their voices for a specific purpose.

• Hounds, such as beagles, foxhounds, bloodhounds, and basset hounds, use their voices a lot because they were bred to call back to their masters during a hunt. The baying call of a beagle and the mournful howl of a bloodhound are particularly penetrating and persistent.

• Herding dogs like Australian kelpies and Shetland sheepdogs were bred to use barking as a way of controlling their flocks.

• Terriers, such as miniature schnauzers and Jack Russells, were bred to alert their owners to the presence of rodents by barking.

• Toy breeds such as Pomeranians, Pekingese, and toy poodles were bred to be lap dogs, so their propensity for barking is a little unusual. They're feisty little things, however, and they bark a lot to show they have big spirits.

"I'd better chase it—or at least bark at it." This type of bark is usually accompanied by confident body language, such as a raised tail or perked-up ears.

Some dogs give this kind of bark when they see something they don't recognize—anything from a person wearing a slicker or a vacuum cleaner in the living room to the sight of their own reflection in a mirror. "You might see the same pattern of lunging forward and then backing up that you would see if your dog were barking at an unfamiliar dog," says Dr. Jones.

High-Pitched

Dogs who want something will often ask for it with an ear-splitting yap. The usual pattern is to bark once, wait a moment to see what happens, then bark again if they're not satisfied. Or they'll give a whole series of high-pitched barks to get your attention. In either case, the barking will usually be accompanied by tail-wagging or other playful signs, says Terry Ryan, a trainer in Sequim, Washington, and author of *The Toolbox for Remodeling Your Problem Dog*.

High-Pitched and Urgent

Just as some people try to relieve anxiety by pacing, some dogs resort to rapid, high-pitched, desperate-sounding barks. "Barking is a definite tension reliever," says Dr. Jones. "It's like primal-scream therapy for dogs."

Some types of dog are especially likely to bark when they're feeling lonely, says Dr. Jones. These include sociable dogs such as beagles, herding dogs such as collies, and breeds that were designed solely to be companion dogs, like most of the toy breeds.

CHAPTER EIGHT

BARKING BACK

People aren't very good at dogspeak, but sometimes giving a growl or a yelp conveys a clearer message than human speech can. And an occasional howl tells your dog that you appreciate him.

No matter how hard they try, dogs will never be proficient in English. Most of what they hear from us comes across as just noise, which is why owners occasionally try to turn things around by communicating in barks, howls, or whines.

It's unlikely anyone will ever publish a *Berlitz Guide to Canine Chat*, if only because speaking dog is a lot more complicated than mastering a foreign language. For one thing, dogs really don't communicate with their voices very much. They depend instead on nonverbal language such as posture, gestures, and scent. Since they don't have a well-defined vocabulary the way humans do, there isn't a bark equivalent for "go outside" or "get your leash." In addition, human vocal cords can't accurately reproduce the sounds of canine speech. Even if you growled to warn your dog off the couch or barked to get his attention, the message wouldn't get through.

"Most dogs would laugh at us if we barked at them," adds Liz Palika, a dog trainer in Oceanside, California. "Their hearing is so much better than ours that we couldn't possibly do justice to their different barking tones."

This doesn't mean dogs won't respond when you imitate a bark. They may bark back or at least look interested for a moment—but it's not

because you accidentally delivered a decipherable message. It's because they're responding to your body language, the tone of your voice, and your overall level of enthusiasm, says Joanne Howl, D.V.M., a veterinarian in private practice in West River, Maryland. "Some people I know do bark, but it is not very effective," she says. "Our dog accent is so atrocious that we ruin their language."

All in the Tone

Even though barking, yelping, howling, whinning, or growling will never replace training or other forms of nonverbal communication, there are situations in

This golden retriever is responding to her owner's tone of voice and body language. Some people try barking at dogs, which gets their attention but doesn't mean much.

which speaking dog, however poorly, allows you to deliver messages that otherwise might get missed. The idea isn't to learn specific barks, but to use some of the same tones and inflections that dogs respond to, says John C. Wright, Ph.D., a certified applied animal behaviorist, professor of psychology at Mercer University in Macon, Georgia, and author of *The Dog Who Would Be King.*

Growling. Dogs that are angry will sometimes respond with a long, low growl. Among canines, it's mainly the high-ranking dogs who growl, while other, more subordinate dogs are less assertive. As a result, dogs are conditioned to equate growls with leadership.

People can take advantage of this when it's time to convey the voice of authority. When dogs are doing something they shouldn't,

Dogs howl to communicate over long distances, but this Labrador cross and his owner are having a howling session just for the fun of it.

giving a low, simmering growl will put them on notice that the "top dog"—meaning you—isn't pleased. You don't have to growl to get results, Dr. Wright adds. Dropping your voice and saying "heyyy" in a low, extended tone will give the same message. "They are prepared to hear a low pitch as a growl," he explains.

Avoid growling too often. Dogs with a tendency to be aggressive or dominant may perceive growls as a direct threat and respond with growls—or worse—of their own. It's also too severe a message for minor problems, like disagreements about getting on the furniture.

Growling is appropriate when you're dealing with puppies, Palika says. They know that their job is to obey their mother or other adults, and a growl is immediately understood.

Howling. In the days when dogs lived far apart, howling was the equivalent of sending up smoke signals. "Where are you?" might be answered by "We're over here." Experts aren't sure if howls actually mean anything or if they're just a convenient way to communicate over long distances. And there's no way to tell if howling at a dog does anything more than get his attention. But dogs may appreciate a howl from their owners, if only because they may view it as a valiant effort to be social, says Dr. Wright.

Yelping. Puppies quickly learn to soften their bites during play-fights when a littermate responds with a yelp. Yelping is a very effective way to help a pup understand that he's biting too much or too hard. "It means, 'Stop, you're hurting me, you're being too rough,'" Dr. Wright explains.

CHAPTER NINE

WORDS EVERY DOG SHOULD KNOW

Dogs will never be gifted linguists but they can learn more than we give them credit for.

Apart from knowing their names, a few basic commands, and really exciting words like "walk" or "biscuit," most dogs are at a loss when it comes to humanspeak. It's not that they're not capable of learning more words. It's just that most people don't feel it's important enough to teach them. But teaching your dog a range of commands has advantages for both of you—your dog will be better to live with, and he'll get a real kick out of doing things that please you.

"Your dog's ability to learn vocabulary is unlimited," says Liz Palika, a dog trainer in Oceanside, California. Her Australian shepherd Ursa learned more than 150 words during her 13 years. When pulling a wagon, Ursa even understood how to follow directions, such as "pull easy," "pull hard," "pull fast," "go left," "turn right," and "make a U-turn."

"Since I was often behind her or had my hands full, she couldn't see me or read my hand gestures," Palika says. "She had to rely on my voice and words."

Ursa was more than just a good wagon dog. She also knew commands like "find the car keys," "take this screwdriver to Paul," and "give me the TV remote."

With patience, dogs can be taught almost any word. This Labrador has learned what "football" means.

Basic Vocabulary

Most dogs, of course, are never going to be Scrabble champions, and while many owners would be thrilled to expand their dogs' vocabu-

laries, they'd settle for a modest six or eight words rather than hundreds. Which words you choose are up to you, although every dog should know the basic five: "sit," "stay," "come," "heel," and "down."

Dogs who know basic obedience commands are a lot easier to be around, Palika says. They feel more secure because they know exactly what you're saying, and they're less likely to steamroll over you the second you open the door or ignore you because they're chasing a squirrel down the block.

The words themselves aren't really important, Palika adds, as long as your dog gets the same message. One of her students, for example, owned an Italian restaurant and used variations of pasta words as commands. Lasagna meant "heel," for example, and linguine meant "stay." "It's a neat trick as long as he doesn't forget what pasta dish meant what command," says Palika. "If his dog zipped out the front gate, he would have to remember to shout 'spaghetti', or the dog wouldn't stop."

Beyond the Basics

Dogs are both attentive and eager to please. They're capable of learning new words very quickly, and many owners decide to keep teaching them new ones. It's satisfying when a dog sits or lies down on command, but it's a lot more fun when he understands expressions such as "wave goodbye."

Teaching words isn't difficult as long as you're patient and take the time to clearly link words with actions, Palika says. Here are some tips for effective training.

Train when he's relaxed. Do your training when your dog is relaxed, but not sleepy—after a good walk, for example.

Use some treats. Start your training by holding in your hand something your dog loves. It can be a dog biscuit, a tennis ball, or anything else that will get his attention. Use the reward to draw his attention where you want it to be. Suppose you're teaching your dog to retrieve the remote control. Put it on the floor in front of him, then use the treat to guide his nose downward while saying "get the remote." When he gives the remote a sniff or nudge, praise him and give him the reward. Then repeat it four or five times.

Make it fun. Dogs learn best when they're having fun, so make training sessions seem like play rather than work. As long as your dog understands that doing something gets you excited, he'll want to keep doing it. Once he's

With a vocabulary that contains more than just the basic words, dogs like this golden retriever can enjoy advanced activities such as agility exercises.

EXTRA CREDIT

Some dogs pick up new words as readily as they pick up bones. If your dog is unusually gifted, you may want try some serious vocabulary-building. For example:

• *Scratch my back.* Nothing soothes a middle-of-the-back itch like a friendly clawed paw. Encourage your dog to paw your back while saying "scratch." When he does, reward him with a treat and hearty praise.

• *Take out the trash.* Most dogs want jobs, and how many people actually jump at this task? Buy plastic trash bags with a handle. Use food to encourage your dog to grab the handle, then give him a lot of praise. Once he gets the hang of grabbing the bag, start escorting him to the curb and praising him some more.

• *Find the sports section.* A newspaper's sections appear in the same order every day. Lay out the sections in their usual order, then point to the sports section. He'll learn to ignore national and local news and go straight to the scores.

• *Find ESPN.* Give your index finger a rest from the remote and let your dog channel-surf. Get him to paw at the control, again by encouraging him with food. If he gets lucky enough to paw the right channel, praise the heck of out of him.

• *Tell them I'm not interested.* Having your dog bark on command is a great way to stop spiels from insistent phone solicitors. See page 117 for information on teaching dogs to bark.

• *Wake me up at 6:00 A.M.* Who needs a bone-jarring alarm clock when a face-licking tail-wagger is available? Dogs crave routine, and they have clocks in their brains that tell them when to wake up. Giving your dog a treat when he comes to the bed and licks your face almost guarantees a repeat performance.

learned the words, your tone of voice won't matter all that much, says John C. Wright, Ph.D., a certified applied animal behaviorist, professor of psychology at Mercer University in Macon, Georgia, and author of *The Dog Who Would Be King.*

Praise the good, ignore the bad. Dogs learn best when they're praised for doing things right. They tune out when they're punished for doing things wrong, says Dr. Wright.

Be consistent. Some dogs learn difficult commands in a few hours, while others may take weeks. But all dogs learn best with repetition. If you practice the commands a few times a day, they'll gradually begin to link the words with the action and the action with the reward. "Anything rewarded consistently with a dog will get done consistently," says Jeff Nichol, D.V.M., a veterinarian in private practice in Albuquerque, New Mexico.

PART THREE

READING BODY LANGUAGE

Dogs depend on body language to an amazing extent.
How they stand, the inclination of their heads, the degree of eye contact,
the set of their ears, and the movements of their tails all speak volumes.
Once you start looking at body language, you'll have a much
better sense for what dogs are saying or feeling.

CHAPTER TEN

What His Body Is Telling You

*From their mobile faces to their expressive tails, dogs use
body language to communicate with people and other dogs. You can tell
at a glance what dogs are thinking and feeling.*

People often think that if a dog isn't wagging his tail, then he's probably not saying much. But dogs use their whole bodies to express themselves. It's worth taking some time to watch your dog, and to pay attention to how he moves and how he looks when reacting to different situations. When you become familiar with his signals—a crouch, flattened ears, or an attentive, cocked head, for example—you'll understand him better, and that will make living together more harmonious for both of you.

Dogs use body language to convey a full range of emotions, wants, and needs, and to express their place within their society. A dog's society is his pack. In the wild, a pack consists of other dogs, but a pet dog's pack comprises his human owners and any other dogs in the family.

Although a particular body part often signals one meaning—for instance, a wagging tail is usually interpreted as a sign of happiness—you need to see what else is going on to understand the full message. For example, when a dog is bowing down and his tail is wagging, then his whirling tail is a clear signal of happiness. But if he's lying on his back, with his eyes and head averted and his front paws folded close to his chest, a moving tail is definitely not a sign that he's happy. Instead, he's showing submission and probably some fear, and is asking for a little kindness and consideration.

Dogs use their whole bodies, from their tongues to the tips of their tails, to express their feelings. This golden retriever is alert and interested in what's going on.

READING THE SIGNS

When someone gets lost in Alaska's millions of acres of wilderness or caught in an avalanche, the Alaska Search and Rescue Dogs are called in. It's not just the dogs' superior senses that help save lives; their handlers need to be able to tell what their dogs are thinking and feeling and to develop an almost symbiotic level of communication with them. It's one time when a human is watching and reading his dog's body language as closely as his dog is watching his.

"The dogs are all trained to give us an alert by barking or digging when they find something," says Corey Aist, who works with his Labrador retriever, Bean. When the teams have been out there for several hours, the conditions are rough, and the dogs are tired, their handlers need to watch carefully for more subtle clues. Some of these clues would be imperceptible to less well trained eyes, but when dogs and humans work so closely together, small signals can have an importance out of proportion to their size. The set of a dog's tail or a minute change in the curvature of his nose, for example, can be enough to tell a handler that his dog thinks there's something worth investigating further.

The other important element in the relationship is trust. "You must completely trust your dog to do the work you've asked him to do," says Paul Stoklos, who searches with his German shepherd, Arrow. "Even if you feel sure he's headed in the wrong direction, follow him anyway."

That's how Stoklos and Arrow once found a man who had become separated from his family in the Alaskan wilderness. Hours of searching with dogs and four-wheel-drive vehicles proved futile—until Arrow became interested in an old poacher's trail. The man's family said he would never have made the mistake of going in that direction, but Arrow was clearly determined to check. Stoklos followed him, and far down the trail, they heard the man's shouts for help. "If I hadn't trusted Arrow, we might never have saved the man's life," says Stoklos.

Some dogs are worse at signaling than other breeds. Tails are invaluable for signaling, so any dog without one is at a disadvantage. Rottweilers, for example, have docked tails. They've also been bred to have big shoulders and an imposing posture. They have trouble showing submission because cringing and making themselves look small isn't an option.

By contrast to their domesticated cousins, all species of wild dogs have shapes and colorings that are well-adapted to signaling. They have short hair that doesn't mask their body language, stiff guard hairs along their backs that they can raise in warning, reasonably distinct facial markings that highlight their expressions, and white underbellies that emphasize their submissive pose when they roll onto their backs.

Reading Your Dog's Emotions

Many canine expressions and gestures such as a hard stare or a nudge are easy to interpret and give us a very straightforward insight into how dogs are feeling, says Ian Dunbar, Ph.D., a behaviorist and the author of *Dog Behavior*. Other gestures, such as tongue-flicking, scratching, shaking, or yawning, have

meanings that aren't so obvious. The more you learn about body language, the more you will understand about what your dog is feeling.

Dogs use body language as a natural part of daily life. They don't stop to think about what they're saying and how they're saying it. Their body language happens spontaneously—and it's happening much of the time.

Old English sheepdogs have difficulty sending clear messages. They can't raise their hackles because their hair is too soft to stand on end, and their stares are invisible.

BODY POSITIONS

Dogs do nearly all of their communicating with body language. Some of the messages are easier to understand than others, but with a little practice, you'll soon be able to translate all your dog's messages.

▶ Saying hello

When dogs greet their owners or another human friend, they often bark happily, hold their tails high and wag them, and race toward the person. Often, as a dog nears his owner, he'll begin to signal his lower status by crouching, lowering his wagging tail, or rolling over, says Michael W. Fox, Ph.D., author of *Understanding Your Dog*.

When greeting each other, dogs use a slightly different approach. They posture to each other as they approach sideways and begin circling. They'll usually stand erect, on tiptoes, with upright ears and tails held high. They'll sniff each other's faces and rear ends to gain vital information about each other's sex, status, and mood. Familiar dogs spend less time sniffing than do dogs who are strangers. If one dog is obviously more dominant, that dog will appear to grow larger, while the subordinate dog will seem to shrink. One dog might put his head or paw on the other's shoulder in an attempt to establish dominance.

If it's not obvious which dog is dominant, they'll jostle side by side, with one trying to place his chin on the other's shoulder. Often the posturing will continue until they accept each other as equals. Dog friends who consider themselves equals will greet each other using quick motions, moving fast, spinning in circles, and jumping up on each other. Acquaintances (but not friends) will sniff each other, and the subordinate dog will lower himself to the other. Sometimes he'll lick the dominant dog's muzzle and raise a front paw to him in an appeasing gesture. Once the posturing is over and accepted, the dogs may sniff and jump on each other before getting down to the fun stuff of romping.

(continued)

BODY POSITIONS—CONTINUED

▼ Happy, calm, and relaxed

When dogs feel relaxed and contented, their whole bodies radiate their happiness. Relaxed dogs stand with all four feet placed evenly on the ground. If they're sitting or lying down, their bodies will assume an easy posture, their muscles free of tension. Dogs with pricked ears will let them relax and fall slightly outwards. Those with floppy ears will let them hang gently or allow the tips of their ears to flop forward. Their heads will be at a comfortable height, neither high nor low, and their foreheads will be smooth. Their mouths will be relaxed at the corners, and either closed or partly open, as though they're smiling. Their tails may be still or wagging slowly. The position of the tail will depend on the breed. Some dogs, such as Afghans, hold their tails very low when they're relaxed, while others, like fox terriers and Airedales, hold them high.

▶ Playful

When dogs want to play with their owners, or when they're asking another dog to play, they'll lower the front halves of their bodies to the ground. Their rear ends will be left pointing in the air, so that it looks as though they're bowing, and their tails will be waving madly in anticipation. They may lower their heads, with their mouths and lips relaxed, and they may pant. Sometimes they'll give a high-pitched bark. They'll prick their ears up alertly and point them forward or, if they have hanging ears, they'll hold them as high and far forward as they can manage.

When their play invitation is answered, dogs will bounce up and down and may bark in excitement. Once play is under way, their exuberant body language, from their pricked-up ears to the jaunty set of their tails, expresses their happiness.

◀ Interested and alert

When dogs go from being calm and relaxed to being interested in something, all parts of their bodies move up and forward. They'll raise their heads and prick their ears up and forward. They'll lean forward slightly, and their mouths may open a little. Their eyes will be bright and intent. A front paw may come up, as though they're getting ready for action.

(continued)

51

BODY POSITIONS—CONTINUED

◀ Bored

Dogs who are confined in restricted spaces without any mental stimulation will soon become bored. They'll look uninterested and morose, with their ears drooping and their eyes set in blank, glassy stares. They'll usually be flat out on the floor, often with their heads resting on their front legs, and their tails limp. Dogs can shake off their boredom and gloomy demeanor the instant they're presented with something fun or interesting to do.

▶ Excited

Dogs usually get excited when they're playing with another dog, greeting a human friend, or it's time to go for a walk or play a game. Excited dogs often show their feelings very clearly by jumping about, or they may stand quivering, with their tails wagging furiously. Often their ears will be held forward in anticipation of something enjoyable, and their eyes will shine with happiness.

When they're greeting their owners, they'll likely rush toward them with their heads held up and their tails wagging, and start nudging them. They may hold their ears back, not as a sign of fear, but as a mark of respectful submission to their leaders.

▶ Sad

A sad dog has the body language of submission. Much like a sad person, he looks thoroughly dejected. He'll hang his head and his tail will be limp.

Dogs rarely become sad unless they're left alone for long periods. Once they're given some attention, exercise, or mental stimulation, they'll usually become relaxed and happy again.

▲ Stalking

When dogs become actively interested in something and decide to hunt, stalk, or play with it, they may lower their heads slightly as they watch it. This is particularly common in hunting or herding breeds, who are bred for this kind of activity. The front halves of their bodies will also be lowered as they stalk, while their rear ends will remain up. They'll watch the object of their interest with a sharp and unwavering gaze. Even when they're standing still, their feet will be positioned so that they can take off suddenly if need be.

(continued)

53

BODY POSITIONS—CONTINUED

◄ Protective

When dogs take it upon themselves to guard and protect what they see as theirs, their body language will start out looking much the same as that of alert and dominant dogs. If they're challenged, though, they'll begin giving out some unmistakably aggressive signals—baring their teeth, thrusting their heads up and forward, and staring boldly to show that they're equal to and ready for the challenge. They'll lean forward to make themselves look bigger than they really are, and their legs will be placed firmly to make it clear that they're standing their ground.

► Aggressive

Dogs who are feeling aggressive or who are on the offensive will make their whole bodies rise and move forward so that they look larger, stronger, and more formidable. They'll lean forward on tiptoes and raise their hackles (the hair on their shoulders and back), which is another effective way of appearing bigger. Their tails will be up and held still, and the hair on the tail may bristle. Their ears will be up and forward. They may be snarling, with their noses wrinkled, the corners of their mouths pushed forward, and their lips tight and tense. Their eyes will be staring—direct and hard. As the aggression escalates, they'll pull their lips back to bare their teeth and will spread their back feet slightly to brace themselves so that they can leap up to fight.

▶ Seeking attention

Dogs are very gregarious animals. They like to be touched, played with, and just hang out with their owners. They enjoy walks immensely, not only for the exercise and the stimulation of the various sights and smells they encounter but also for the human companionship. And because dogs are so sociable, they spend quite a bit of time asking their owners for attention.

A paw on a person's knee can sometimes be a dominant gesture from an assertive dog or an appeasing gesture from a more submissive one—but most of the time, it's just a way of saying, "I'd like some attention, please!" Pawing the air in front of someone serves the same purpose, as does sliding a head under his hand and jostling it or standing up and leaning on his leg.

Other common attention-seeking tactics that dogs employ include nudging aside a newspaper or book that a person is reading, scrabbling noisily on the floor as though they're digging, and nudging or headbutting someone.

(continued)

Body Positions—Continued

▼ Dominant

Dominant dogs stand tall. When dogs meet, they'll raise their heads and lift their tails. They'll make themselves look larger by raising the hair along their spines and on their shoulders. They may stand on the tips of their front toes and take one or two small, stiff-legged steps forward. Their ears will be forward and as upright as their natural shape and position allow. One dog may put his paw on the shoulder of the other to reinforce his dominance. Unless the other dog begins to show submissive signals, the two dogs may resolve the power struggle with a fight.

Mounting or other sexual behaviors aren't always associated with reproduction. Dogs will sometimes mount other dogs to express dominance. Both the mounter and the mountee can be either male or female. Mounting and other sexual behaviors are the ultimate in disrespect when dogs try to perform them on their owners.

It's common for dogs to greet people by jumping up on them and trying to lick their faces. Dogs who jump on their owners and also have erect tails and stiff ears are trying to convey dominance.

▶ Submissive

Submissive dogs always try to make themselves appear smaller. It's a way of saying, "I'm no challenge, so please don't hurt me." They'll crouch or cower, with their backs arched and their heads pulled in and lowered. Their ears will be pulled down and back, and their foreheads smooth. They won't make eye contact and may in fact avert their eyes. They'll pull back the corners of their mouths and may look to be smiling, although this isn't a smile as we know it. They may also lick their noses. Their tails will be down and perhaps pulled up tightly between their back legs. And the tips of their tails may be wagging or twitching. They may make pawing movements with their front feet.

When they're with a more dominant dog, they'll sometimes lick his muzzle, or lift a front paw to him to show that they acknowledge who's in charge. Other times they'll show their acceptance of the status quo by licking their own noses and putting their ears back—either slightly or flat to their skulls. If their ears are flat to their skulls, they're accepting a reprimand; if their ears waver back and forth, or one is higher than the other, they're also accepting it, but with a fair degree of reluctance. If they're totally obedient, they'll also tuck their tails between their legs.

In extreme submission, dogs lie down, roll over, and bare their bellies. They'll pull their legs in against their bodies, and their front paws will be tucked in close, too. Their tails will be pulled in between their back legs and tucked against their bellies, and the tips of their tails may be twitching. Some dogs will dribble a little urine.

Not all submissive behavior indicates a fearful mood, though. A dog may bare his belly to his owner yet maintain direct, soft eye contact, which shows that he's not afraid. His posture is one of deference and trust. He could also, of course, be angling for a tummy rub.

(continued)

BODY POSITIONS—Continued

▼ Fearful

Dogs who feel frightened but are not moved to behave aggressively will try to make themselves look smaller than they really are. Frightened dogs will lower their heads and lay their ears back. If they're very fearful, their ears will be plastered tight to their heads, and they'll usually avert their gaze from whatever it is that's scared them. Their pupils may be dilated, and they'll sometimes even close their eyes completely in their attempt to cope with the situation. Their mouths will probably be closed, too. The skin on their muzzles may be wrinkled and the corners of their mouths pulled back and down in a tense expression.

Sometimes dogs find themselves in situations where they're afraid, but they feel that they have something to protect—themselves, their humans, or property—and they're prepared to take a stand. When this happens, their body language will convey both fear and aggression. Their bodies will probably be lowered, legs bent, and their heads held forward but low. Their ears may be back, showing fear, or may go back and forth, signaling their conflicting emotions. Some dogs will gaze at what's frightening them, others will look away, and some will show the whites of their eyes. They'll bare their teeth and wrinkle their muzzles—all signs of aggression. Their hackles will be up, their tails low but bristling. A fearful dog who is cornered and is also showing aggressive body language should be taken seriously. He's saying that he's quite prepared to bite.

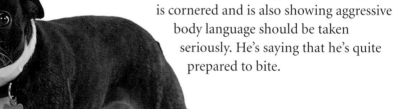

▶ Anxious

When dogs are stressed, they'll lower their heads and pant in a desperate effort to relieve their anxiety. Their pupils will be dilated and they won't be able to look at the person or thing that's causing their distress. Their ears will be down and back, and their lips will also be pulled well back and creased at the corners. They'll hold their bodies low and their tails will be tucked between their back legs. Often their paws will be sweating. Sometimes they'll roll over and bare their bellies, and even express a few drops of urine. Dogs who are sitting still with one paw raised are usually worried or anxious.

▼ Relieving anxiety

Dogs use a number of body language signals to soothe themselves, other dogs, or people they're interacting with, says Terry Ryan, a dog trainer and author of *The Toolbox for*

Remodeling Your Problem Dog. These actions, called calming signals, look to be irrelevant to what's happening at the time, and they're the canine equivalent of the way people will change the subject of a conversation if an argument seems likely to erupt. Some common calming signals include yawning, tongue-flicking, turning away, breaking eye contact, sniffing, scratching, or shaking themselves as though they're wet.

The way to tell that dogs are using calming signals is to look for an action that's out of context. During an obedience-training session, a dog may suddenly scratch at his collar. If he doesn't have fleas and hasn't been scratching during the rest of the session, he's probably trying to relieve stress. He could be saying, "Hey, I need a break from concentrating."

CHAPTER ELEVEN

WHAT YOUR BODY IS TELLING HIM

Dogs watch people more closely than people ever watch them.
You need to pay close attention to your body language so you don't
accidentally send your dog the wrong message.

Had a bad day at the office? Your dog knows as soon as you walk in the door. Just as you can tell what dogs are feeling by their postures and the ways they move their tails, your body language—the hundreds of poses, gestures, and facial expressions you unconsciously use all the time—tells them a lot about your moods and intentions.

Some of these clues are pretty obvious. When you walk into the kitchen or pick up the leash, it doesn't take a canine Einstein to figure out that something good is about to happen. But dogs are also capable of tremendous discrimination. Things people would never notice, like minute shifts in posture or a flicker at the corner of an eye, are instantly noticed and evaluated. Dogs can tell at a glance when you're happy or sad, when you want to play, and when you're annoyed by the tipped-over trash.

"Humans have a wonderful spoken vocabulary that's very extensive, but most of it is a closed book to dogs, so they attach a great deal of importance to physical signs," says Steve Aiken, an animal behaviorist in Wichita, Kansas. They're so attuned to body language, in fact, that they often pick up messages where none

When this Labrador's owner gets down on all fours, she mimics the pose a dog uses to invite play. Her dog knows right away that a game is afoot.

were intended. Many household misunderstandings could be avoided if people were a little more conscious of the signals they send.

Here's a common scenario: You're down on all fours, desperately searching for a dropped wedding band or an essential screw, and your dog is driving you crazy by jumping on your back, running in circles, and barking his head off. Play is the last thing you have in mind, so you snap and shove him away, and he slinks off looking disappointed. He misinterpreted your mood, but there's a good reason for it. When a dog wants another dog to play, he'll often crouch down and put his tail in the air. It's called a play-bow, and that's exactly what he thought you were doing, says Melissa Shyan, Ph.D., an animal behaviorist and associate professor of psychology at Butler University in Indianapolis, Indiana.

Here's another example: When people have difficult conversations on the telephone, their voices get a little raspy, or their breathing gets labored or shallow. Dogs recognize the signs of stress and will sometimes get a little anxious themselves, especially if they think their owners are stressed because of them. If this happens a few times, they may begin to associate the telephone itself with anxiety and will start getting upset whenever their owners pick it up.

It isn't practical (or necessary) to constantly worry about how your dog is interpreting your facial expressions or body language. Most dogs roll with the punches just like people do, and a little misunderstanding isn't likely to bother them for long. But if you suspect that your dog's behavior has changed because of something you've done, it's worth paying attention to the types of signals you've been sending out. "It's up to you to give your dog feedback if you think he's misunderstood your body language," says Deena Case-Pall, Ph.D., a psychologist and animal behaviorist in Camarillo, California. "Otherwise he'll keep associating the same act with his first impression."

Canine on Patrol

PUPPY DOG TALES

There are few dogs more highly trained than those that accompany police officers on duty. The National K-9 Training School in Columbus, Ohio, trains many dogs for police work every year. K-9 units have been established in police departments throughout the United States.

It's not just the intense training that makes these dogs so effective, though. It's also the focus on their owners. Many police dogs live with their police officer handlers around the clock.

Curt Larsen, a K-9 officer for the City of Poughkeepsie, New York, spends as much or more time with his German shepherd, CheeBee, than he does with his family—and CheeBee's good work is the proof.

"When we're out patrolling the streets, he acts just like any other dog, looking out of the window, enjoying the view," explains Larsen. "But he can tell when something is about to happen just by the way I hold myself and the way I drive. If I speed up and reach for the lights, CheeBee is ready for action. He looks straight ahead, he gets more rigid, and his ears go up."

CheeBee can also tell when Larsen's interactions with people on the street are likely to be friendly or not. "He can tell by my demeanor whether or not he needs to worry," says Larsen. "He knows hand-shaking and pats on the back are okay. But once, when I found drugs on a guy, the guy pushed me, and CheeBee flew out of the car and grabbed hold of him."

How Dogs Learn to Read Us

Just as children quickly learn to pick up clues from their parents, dogs understand the wisdom of watching their owners. After all, people are the ones who dole out food. They control the door that leads to the backyard. They're the ones who decide when it's time to play and when to be stern. Dogs enjoy life best when it's predictable, and there's no surer way to predict what's about to happen than by watching their owners' silent signals. Over time, dogs get remarkably adept at reading and interpreting these signals. They have an almost uncanny ability to know what's coming. In some cases, in fact, they know what you're about to do even before you do.

Since this type of "mind-reading" can only enhance the bond between people and pets, Aiken recommends encouraging it whenever you can. The next time your dog quickly moves out of the way when you make the slightest turn in his direction, reward him for his skill in anticipating your movement, he advises. This will make him even more determined to scrutinize you closely. He'll gradually sharpen his powers of observation and will seldom be taken by surprise.

Observation comes naturally to dogs. They used to live in large groups called packs, and it was essential for every dog in the pack to know what the others were doing and what their movements signified. In the thousands of years that dogs have been domesticated, they've undoubtedly lost many of their survival instincts—but not the power of observation because it's a skill that continues to be helpful today.

BREED SPECIFIC

Some breeds are better at reading body signals than others. Herding breeds, such as Border collies, corgis (below), and Australian kelpies, were bred to pay close attention to cattle and sheep so they could predict their movements.

These dogs got many of their instructions from hand signals, so they always paid careful attention to body language. These instincts remain so strong that even their nonherding contemporaries feel compelled to keep an eye on what's happening.

Dogs' senses are incredibly sharp but their interpretations of human movements and facial expressions are somewhat limited. No matter how attentive dogs are, it's impossible for them to truly think like a person. They have to draw on their skills in communicating within their own species to interpret our movements and patterns of behavior, explains Barbara Simpson, Ph.D., a veterinary behaviorist in Southern Pines, North Carolina. As a result, they focus mainly on signals that are similar to those used by dogs or those that they think may play a role in survival. "Dogs remember situations in which they've been hurt, and they watch out to make sure that they don't happen again," says Dr. Shyan. "But mostly they just want to have a great time, so they watch us for signs that something's going to happen that will make their lives happier."

Using Body Language Effectively

Dogs will never be adept at learning English or sign language, and humans will never learn to communicate as expressively as dogs using body language. But it's generally not that difficult to use your body, face, and hand movements to communicate messages a little more clearly—or at least to avoid sending the wrong signals that dogs are sure to misunderstand.

Posture

People who stand proudly with their shoulders back and their heads erect are sending the world a silent message that says "I'm confident."

This golden retriever is enjoying a pat on the head from his owner, but if a stranger did the same thing, he might feel uneasy.

People respect those who are self-assured and confident, and so do dogs.

Combine a confident posture with a brisk, self-assured walk, and dogs quickly assume that this person is powerful and in charge and will take care of everything. They respond immediately because they've seen confident dogs—who have tremendous status among their peers—act in a similar way.

Hand and Arm Movements

People use their hands and arms a lot when they're talking or feeling emotional, and we intuitively understand what different movements mean. Holding your hand over the top of someone's head, for example, makes that person feels vaguely threatened, while standing with your arms opened wide makes you appear friendly and inviting. Dogs react to both types of gestures in a similar way. They dislike it when people they don't know reach down to pet their heads. Among dogs, this type of reaching down is considered provocative, even an invitation to fight. Open arms, on the other hand, are similar to the spread-eagled, flat-on-the-back position dogs assume when they're playing or feeling relaxed. People with an "open" position are seen as being friendly and unthreatening.

Quick hand movements may scare or aggravate dogs. In centuries past, fast-moving objects were either dinner or aggressors, says Dr. Shyan. This is why dogs instantly get alert when we move our bodies quickly. They feel much more relaxed when we move our hands slowly and deliberately.

Some people go a bit overboard with body language when they're greeting dogs they don't

This collie sees his owner's open arms as offering a big welcome, so he's eager to come on command.

know. They'll shove their hands out for dogs to sniff or wave their arms around to show they're happy and enthusiastic. It's not the movements themselves that are the problem so much as the speed and force with which they occur. Dogs are naturally a little nervous around strangers, and forceful gestures may be interpreted as threatening—and dogs may react accordingly.

Quick or Jerky Movements

When two dogs are squaring off for a confrontation, they'll stiffen and stand tall, and their movements will be jerky and nervous. "Dogs pick up on anything that seems abnormal or worrying in our movements, too," says Aiken. "If someone is at the front door and you make jerky motions because you're uneasy, your dog will pick up on that and think right away something is wrong." When you move slowly, however, they know you're calm and relaxed, and they'll relax too.

"Every dog reacts differently depending on his personality, but most dogs will be startled if their owner suddenly launches into an exercise routine or has a wrestling game with

someone else," says Bill Wolden, an instructor at the exotic animal training and management program at Moorpark College in Moorpark, California. "Many dogs feel threatened and become alarmed until they've had a chance to figure out what's happening. They feel much more comfortable when you're going at a slow speed."

Facial Expressions

Happy dogs and happy people have smooth foreheads and give easy eye contact. Angry dogs and angry people have furrowed brows and sometimes a hard, fixed stare. But that's where the similarities end: A human smile and a canine smile mean entirely different things.

People smile when they're happy. Dogs, on the other hand, smile—it's really more like a grin—when they're afraid. They'll raise their upper lip and bare their teeth, which looks very menacing. It's their way of scaring off whatever it is they're afraid of. Trainers recommend keeping your mouth closed, or at least being careful not to show too many teeth, when you're greeting a strange dog who looks tense and alert. Smiling may make him think you're being threatening, and he may get aggressive in return.

"Most dogs learn very quickly that a human smile is a good thing," adds Mary Welther, a dog trainer in San Diego. "The body language that goes with a human smile helps them understand this, and they learn to react in a positive manner. If a dog is unsure about something and you smile at him, he'll come to understand that you approve of what he's doing."

Move as Dogs Do

Miscommunication is most common among strangers. Once you've spent a few years with a dog, the two of you have pretty much figured out each other's body language and there aren't too many surprises. When a new or unfamiliar dog comes along, however, body language that speaks volumes to your own dog may be greeted with confusion, blank stares, or worse. It's worth knowing a little universal dog language to make the introductions more friendly.

PAY ATTENTION

Every dog can be taught to be more attentive. Herding dogs need little encouragement, but most dogs lose their focus fairly easily. One way to keep them alert and attentive is by teaching the "watch me" command.

1 Hold a treat in one hand. Have your dog sit in front of you and let him sniff the treat. Tell him "Watch me!" and raise the treat from his nose to your chin. As he watches the treat, watch his eyes.

2 When his eyes flick to your face, tell him "Good dog to watch me!" and give him the treat. Practice two or three more times and then take a break. Repeat the exercise several times. As he progresses, make it more challenging. Have him watch for longer periods or move about as he watches you. Then, when you want to teach him something new, you can use the "watch me" command first to make sure he's paying attention.

Get down to their level. Since dogs sometimes use their height, which they exaggerate by stretching their legs and craning their necks upward, in order to intimidate other dogs, they assume that people do the same thing, and may get affronted when you approach and loom over them.

A friendlier greeting is one in which you get down to their level, either by kneeling or by slowly bending over. The lower you go, the bigger dogs feel, and that can make them feel more secure and less threatened. It's also a good idea to extend your hand slightly so they can give a quick sniff without getting too close. "Dogs will sniff a stranger to figure out what he is all about," Wolden explains.

Take care with a stare. Dogs certainly don't mind looking into their owners' eyes, but a direct stare, especially from a stranger, is considered very offensive as well as aggressive. It's okay to look at a strange dog's eyes to see how he reacts, but don't hold your gaze for more than a second. (If a dog is growling or otherwise acting aggressively, avoid eye contact entirely.) It's better to avert your gaze and look just past him when you meet for the first time. Or you can lower your eyes when he tries to make eye contact, which is a way of saying "I'm not a threat, so you can relax."

Approach him sideways. Dogs greet one another by sniffing hindquarters, which involves a sideways approach. You certainly don't want to imitate the greeting, but approaching sideways is a good way to make friends because among dogs it's considered good manners. Walking straight toward a dog will make him uncomfortable, and he may mis-

take your friendly attentions for something more threatening.

Leave your emotions at the office. There's no avoiding bad days, but the same emotions that rile you can make dogs extremely nervous. When you bang open the door and stomp into the house, your dog will quickly assume that he's in for a tense evening. Worse, he'll likely assume that you're mad because of something he did. "You'd be just as keyed up if someone came rushing into your domain," says Aiken. You can't force yourself into a good mood, but it's worth pausing in the driveway to imagine your home-coming from your dog's point of view.

The owner of this Labrador cross tries to leave her worries at the door so that she gives him a warm and friendly greeting.

CHAPTER TWELVE

FACE

Dogs can't put on a happy face when they're feeling blue.
And they can't change the natural look of their breed either.
So their state of mind is usually easy to ascertain.

We can read people's moods to a certain extent from the set of their facial features. But people have the ability to consciously mask their feelings, composing their faces to say one thing when their minds are saying something different. Dogs have many distinct facial expressions and usually it's pretty clear whether they're happy or sad, angry or content. Though they don't deliberately set out to deceive or dissemble in the way humans do, the natural appearance of their breed, or their mix of breeds, can cause confusion. Markings, coloring, the shape of the head or the eyes are something a dog can do nothing about. But because we persist in associating a mood with these immutable looks, miscommunications can occur.

Many dog owners choose a breed of dog entirely on the strength of a perceived personality that is related to the breed's natural expression. "Golden retrievers always look like they're very happy, and I wanted a happy dog, not a serious one," says Nancy Hoffman of Oceanside, California. Labrador retrievers, Alaskan malamutes, and Samoyeds also always seem to have cheerful facial expressions.

Other breeds give different impressions. Australian cattle dogs and Border collies have

Everything about this golden retriever's face says he hasn't a care in the world.

upright ears and an intense gaze, and people think they're always on red alert, ready for action. Pugs, with their short muzzles, black facial coloring, and large eyes, seem anxious or studious. Although these expressions do portray something of each breed's natural personality, it's not always the whole picture. Not all pugs are permanently on the brink of an anxiety attack, just as not all golden retrievers are always sublimely happy.

67

The positioning of dogs' heads and ears works in tandem with facial expressions to give us helpful clues about what state of mind our dogs are in. When dogs hear or see something they find unusual, they'll move their ears up and forward and cock their heads to the side. Combined with the alert and intent look on their faces, this makes their expressions appear even more quizzical. "There are nuances in facial expressions that must be watched carefully if we're to understand our dogs as best we can," says Mary Stout, a trainer in San Diego, California. "A twitch of an ear, the lifting of the lip, the tilt of the head, and the furrowing of the forehead all have significance and something to say."

Structural Variations

Although most dogs' facial features play a very important part in their ability to communicate, not all dogs are created equal when it comes to having the tools to express themselves easily or clearly. Sometimes a dog's body type or breed characteristics limit his facial repertoire.

Nearly all facial expressions, for example, include some kind of movement of a dog's mouth or lips. Breeds like bloodhounds with their long, thick, pendulous lips, called flews, have much more difficulty making some of these expressions. Although they can snarl—pulling their lips back and baring their front teeth—other expressions that require more subtle lip movements (especially at the corners of the mouth) are virtually beyond their capabilities, try as they may. And even if they can achieve some of these movements, they can be very hard for the onlooker to discern. Calming gestures such as licking may be particularly hard to see. Also, dogs with long flews have difficulty drawing up the back of the lips to make what people take to be a happy expression. Because of this, we often think these dogs are feeling sad, even when they're not.

EMOTIONS UNDER WRAPS

The facial expressions of short-haired dogs are generally easy to read. But other breeds, such as Old English sheepdogs and Lhasa apsos (below), have luxuriant locks that hide their expressions. Perhaps the most extravagantly hairy dog is the puli, a Hungarian sheepdog whose floor-length dreadlocks can make it difficult to tell front from rear.

So how do these dogs show what they're feeling? Most of them, like Maltese and Shih Tzus, get artificial help—their owners tie their hair back out of their eyes. But pulis don't like direct sunlight in their eyes, so their hair is usually left loose to shield them. Fortunately their eyes and their characteristically happy faces are still visible through their corded coats. And, as pulis are lively and outgoing, they're usually bouncing about enough to flick the hair out of their eyes anyway.

When a dog's repertoire of expressions is restricted, it's important to watch his overall body language to understand what it is he's trying to communicate. Shar-peis, in particular, drew the short straw here. Bred to have meatier, fleshier faces than other breeds, the shar-pei's multitudinous skin folds severely restrict lip expressions and the movement of skin on the muzzle, brow, and around the eyes.

Hair covering can also obscure dogs' facial expressions. Old English sheepdogs, who have thick coats and shaggy hair in their faces, are at a distinct disadvantage here. Almost all their expressions, subtle or obvious, are difficult to see. "When working with a long-coated breed such as the Old English, I watch coat movement," says Stout. "If the hair moves over the eyes, or around the mouth, I assume that the dog is making some kind of an expression. I then watch the rest of his body language to see if I can understand what he's trying to say."

By understanding what your dog's facial expressions signify, you can combine this information with what else his body is telling you. That way you get a complete picture of what he's feeling and trying to say.

Facial Markings and Colorings

Some breeds, such as Doberman pinschers, Australian shepherds, Bernese mountain dogs, Rottweilers, and Japanese chins, have distinctive colorings or markings that draw attention to certain facial features. Tan markings above their eyes and dark lips against a pale muzzle help make their expressions more visible.

Picture a dog with a white muzzle and black lips and eyes surrounded by white fur, with perhaps a touch of tan around or above them. When the dog snarls—lifting his lips, wrinkling his nose, and furrowing his forehead—his coloring makes this expression more pronounced. His black lips are offset by the white muzzle, and his white teeth are outlined by black lips. The lighter colors around his eyes and the tan markings where eyebrows would be also make his intense eyes more obvious.

Even all-white breeds, such as Samoyeds or Great Pyrenees, or pale-faced ones, like Alaskan malamutes, often have dark-rimmed eyes, black noses, and black lips, which make their expressions more visible.

POOCH PUZZLER

Is your dog smiling?

When dogs seem to be smiling, you can't always take their expressions at face value. Some dogs have what's known as a submissive grin, says Ian Dunbar, Ph.D., author of *Dog Behavior*. This grin is actually a snarl, but some dogs do it when they are expressing high emotions—usually aggression, but often happiness and excitement. This expression seems to be breed-related and is often seen in Australian shepherds, Doberman pinschers, Dalmatians, and Border collies.

There's obviously room for confusion when a snarl can be misinterpreted as a smile. The key is to look at the rest of the dog's body language. A smiling dog's body language will be happy, with a wagging tail, while a snarling dog will be tense and aggressive.

69

A Guide to Facial Features

Dogs' facial features work together, and the message they're combining to send isn't hard to understand once you know what to look for. Here's what each feature may be saying.

Ears. Unlike people, dogs have mobile ears that can swivel, lay back, or tilt forward. They also move independently of each other. This range of movement makes their ears very expressive. When a dog's ears are held forward, he's alert; when they're back and relaxed, he's relaxed, too. Forward-facing, tensely erect ears show aggression. Ears folded back tightly show a dog who's afraid and maybe aggressive.

Eyes. A soft and loving look shows affection and trust, and an absence of fear and tension. A direct, eager look indicates interest and alertness. A sideways glance means submission or uncertainty. Rapidly blinking eyes are a reaction to stress and can be a dog's attempt to calm himself down. Direct, hard eye contact sends a message of dominance or aggression.

When the whites of a dog's eyes show, you need to look at other body language clues to work out the cause. When a dog is afraid and his ears are pulled way back, the stretching of the skin may cause the whites to show. However, if a dog is lying on his back for a tummy rub, the whites of his eyes may show simply because gravity is pulling his eyelids back.

Forehead. When the skin on a dog's forehead is relaxed, so is he. When it's smooth and drawn back tightly, that means his ears have been pulled down and back because he's afraid or perhaps aggressive. A dog who's feeling anxious will furrow his forehead over his eyes, just like a knitted human brow.

Mouth. A mouth partly open is a relaxed, normal position for many dogs. It doesn't always signify an emotion, but when it does, the emotion is generally happiness. A panting dog may be nervous or stressed, or maybe he's just hot. If he's licking—another dog, a person, or his own muzzle—that's a sign of greeting or submission. Licking can also be a gesture meant to calm himself, a person, or another dog.

When a dog's teeth are chattering, this isn't a sign that he's cold, but generally indicates happy anticipation. A dog who's expecting an especially good toy or who's in the middle of an exciting play session may chatter his teeth.

Lips. Relaxed lips indicate a relaxed dog. An aggressive dog will pull his lips back tightly in a snarl. A stressed dog will pull his lips way back, creasing the corners of his mouth. In many dogs, the black lips contrast with the color of the muzzle, emphasizing their expressions and the size and whiteness of their teeth.

The contrasting colors on this Bernese mountain dog's face, such as his tan eyebrows and black lips against a white muzzle, draw attention to his expressions and also make them very easy to read.

FACIAL EXPRESSIONS

It's easy to read your dog's face once you understand the subtleties of his expressions. And you can marry this information with other body language clues to gain a deeper understanding of what he's thinking.

◀ Relaxed, happy, and comfortable

Everyone likes to see this expression and, in fact, dogs usually look pretty contented and at peace with the world. A dog who's feeling comfortable and unworried, lying by the fire or out on the porch, will look serene and untroubled. His brow will be smooth and his mouth may be either closed or open in a relaxed position, perhaps with his tongue lolling out.

Playful

When a dog's asking someone to romp with him, he'll make it pretty obvious that he's got fun in mind. "A dog who wants to play will have his eyes wide open, his ears will either be cocked forward or flat, and he may pant or salivate," says Melissa Shyan, Ph.D., an animal behaviorist and associate professor of psychology at Butler University in Indianapolis, Indiana. "He'll look just like a puppy."

▶ Excited and welcoming

A dog who is happily greeting his owner or another human friend, or a puppy who's saying hello to a friendly older dog, will open his mouth slightly and flick his tongue rapidly in and out. He may try to lick the other person or dog, which is a clear sign of respect and affection, or he may lick at the corners of his own mouth.

(continued)

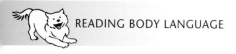

FACIAL EXPRESSIONS—CONTINUED

▶ **Submissive and worried**

A dog who's slightly submissive and a little worried may look indirectly at whatever's worrying him, but he's more likely to look away. That's his way of saying "Please ignore me, I'm no threat." His mouth will usually be closed, but sometimes it will be open and his tongue will appear. It may flick out between his front teeth, which is a sign of nervousness or anxiety. He may also try to lick. This gesture is designed to appease and to assure the other person or dog that he knows his place and respects the other's superior status.

◀ **Interested and curious**

When a dog's interest picks up, so do his facial features. They'll all move up and forward a little. "A curious dog will aim his ears at what he's looking at, and he'll be sniffing the air, hoping to figure out what that unusual scent is," says Dr. Shyan. He may be nudging something with his nose and his mouth may be closed, unless it's a hot day, in which case his mouth will be open all the time. The skin on his forehead may have a tiny wrinkle, but most of the time it will be smooth.

When a dog starts stalking whatever has caught his attention, his facial features will remain up, forward, and intent. He may squint a little, his mouth will be closed, and his ears will be pricked up.

◀ Worried or anxious

Dogs who are worried or stressed will have dilated pupils, open mouths, and they'll pull their lips right back, creasing them at the corners. They may also be panting, which is a sign that they're stressed.

Frightened

Dogs who are frightened don't just pull back with their bodies—they do so with their faces. They'll pull their ears back tightly against their heads and pull their lips down and back. They'll also usually lower their heads and look away from whatever is bothering them.

▶ Watchful and alert

Dogs who are watchful and alert will do the opposite of frightened dogs—their facial features will move up and forward in their eagerness to study what it is that's interesting them. Their eyes will be intense and watchful, and their brow may be furrowed in concentration. The skin around their eyes may be creased, and their mouths slightly agape. The nose will be twitching and their neck muscles will be taut.

(continued)

73

FACIAL EXPRESSIONS—Continued

▶ Aggressive

Aggressive facial expressions start out looking much the same as those of an alert dog. However, when a dog starts feeling that aggression might be called for, his features will become more distorted. He'll begin by lifting his lips at the side of his mouth, to show his sharp canine teeth. If he then thinks the situation calls for a sterner warning, he'll pull his lips right up and bare all his teeth. His forehead will be furrowed, and the skin around his eyes will be deeply creased. His mouth will be open, and he'll probably be growling or barking. He'll also wrinkle the skin over his muzzle—sometimes so much that his nose changes shape.

◀ Conflicting emotions

Dogs are sometimes of mixed minds about things. When a dog's feeling both protective and a little afraid, as a timid dog might when a stranger intrudes on his turf, his facial features will show his conflicting feelings. His ears may be halfway up, showing a degree of boldness, yet held back against his skull, indicating fear. Sometimes his ears end up in a position between the two extremes, which shows his confusion. While drawing his lips up and baring his teeth—a sign of aggression—he may also signal fear by pulling his lips back so that their corners crease. As he bares his teeth, his mouth may be open, not in a tense, aggressive position, but open almost fully. This is what a distressed puppy would do, and adult dogs commonly revert to puppylike actions when they're perturbed.

CHAPTER THIRTEEN

EYES

Dogs don't see the world in the same way people do,
but their eyes are just as expressive, and you can tell a lot about
their state of mind just by looking at their eyes.

Sight is our most important sense, and it's the one we rely on most. But dogs don't depend on their vision that much. They mostly use it to confirm what their other senses tell them, says Craig Larson, D.V.M., a veterinarian in private practice in Santa Barbara, California. For example, dogs may hear their owner's car and dash to the front gate. They're familiar with the sound, so seeing the car simply proves what they already knew. The same thing happens with scent. Dogs smell a scent, know

it's that of a squirrel, and follow the trail. When they flush the squirrel, the sight of it stimulates them to chase it, but doesn't give them any new information. It just confirms what their noses already told them.

When you're trying to communicate with dogs, you need to know how their vision works and how they use it. Once you know this, you'll be able to use visual communication in a way they understand. You'll also realize that if your dog seems to misunderstand you, it may be because he doesn't see things the same way you do.

Canine Eyesight

Dogs' eyes are more sensitive to light and movement than people's are, but they can't focus on things as well. That's why dogs can see very slight movements in dim light, but they sometimes can't see balls a foot away in broad daylight. Even brightly colored balls that contrast vividly with the surroundings won't be much easier for them to see because dogs have poor color vision.

People and dogs have different numbers of receptor cells—called rods and cones—in their eyes. Rods pick up very low levels of light, but only in black and white. Dogs have more rods

POOCH PUZZLER

Why do their eyes shine in the dark?

Catch a dog's eyes in the glare of a flashlight or the headlights of your car at night, and you'll see them shining back at you.

Their eyes glow in the dark because they have a structure behind the retina called the tapetum lucidum. This is a highly reflective layer of cells that gives the eyes a second chance to absorb all the available light, says D. Caroline Coile, Ph.D., a neuroscientist in Ochlocknee, Georgia. The tapetum in dogs is usually greenish yellow, and that's the color you'll see at night.

than we do, which means that in dim light their sight is keener than ours. This is a throwback to their wild days. Prey such as deer are most active at dawn and dusk, so wild dogs needed to be able to see in dim light to have any chance of catching their next meal, says D. Caroline Coile, Ph.D., a neuroscientist in Ochlocknee, Georgia. Cones, on the other hand, are needed to see in daylight and to pick up color. Dogs have fewer of these than people do.

While it used to be thought that dogs saw the world in black and white and shades of gray, like a black and white television set, researchers now know that dogs have some color vision. But recognizing color isn't very important for their daily lives. "They've managed to survive all these years without recognizing all the world's colors," says Wayne Hunthausen, D.V.M., an animal behaviorist and past president of the American Veterinary Society of Animal Behavior in Westwood, Kansas.

BREED SPECIFIC

Greyhounds, whippets, salukis, and borzois are called sighthounds because they hunt by sight rather than scent. They're very attracted to movement, have a strong instinct to chase moving prey, and have better distance vision than other dogs, which means they watch their prey during the hunt.

What does matter to dogs is detecting movement, says Dr. Coile. When dogs were predators, movement was the trigger that made them pay attention because it meant that dinner was nearby. Today's dogs don't need to hunt, but they retain their ancestors' skills and instincts.

Dogs also have a wider field of vision than people do. Their eyes are set wider apart than those of humans, which means dogs can see

COLOR COMBINATIONS

While dogs' eyes mostly come in various shades of brown, it's not uncommon to see other colors or mixtures of colors. Some dogs have mismatched eyes: One eye may be blue and one brown, or one may be brown and the other half brown, half blue. This is common in Siberian huskies, Dalmatians, Australian shepherds, collies, and other breeds with white or merle coats.

Dogs with blue eyes have a missing layer of pigment in the iris. It gives the dogs an unusual look and makes their eyes a little more sensitive to light. But it has no effect on their eyesight. Dogs with blue eyes, however, are more likely to be born deaf: Blue eyes are caused by the same genes that result in white and merle coat colors, and these genes are linked to hearing defects.

more to each side of them. Their field of vision ranges from 190 degrees for flat-faced dogs such as Pekingese to 270 degrees for greyhounds, says Janice da Silva, Ph.D., a veterinary ophthalmologist in La Puente, California. By contrast, humans can only see 180 degrees.

One thing that doesn't vary much between breeds is the size of their eyes. The variation in eyeball volume between Chihuahuas and mastiffs, for example, is a surprisingly tiny 11 percent, which is why toy dogs' eyes tend to bulge.

Some breeds are more prone than others to eye problems. Rough collies, Border collies, and Shetland sheepdogs are sometimes born blind because of a genetic mutation, and breeds with prominent eyes may suffer from exposure keratitis, or wear and tear on the cornea.

When It's Okay to Disobey

Guide dogs are trained to aid people who are blind in all sorts of ways. They take them on public transport and help them get safely through crowds. But sometimes it's what dogs won't do that matters.

Jim Hughes, a high school history teacher in Farmingdale, New York, owes his life to his guide dog, Ronny. Jim was walking with Ronny across a construction site. Suddenly Ronny stopped and refused to go any farther, despite Jim's increasingly exasperated commands to do so. "He wouldn't move," Jim says. "It was as though he was saying, 'No, I won't!'"

Finally, Jim carefully moved one foot forward—and encountered nothing but air. The reason for Ronny's refusal became clear: Obeying Jim would have meant falling into a huge pit. Ronny's good judgment saved Jim from serious injury.

The Seeing Eye guide dog school in Morristown, New Jersey, calls this kind of refusal "intelligent disobedience," and, as Jim can attest, it's the smartest thing a dog can do.

The Meaning of Eye Contact

Dogs communicate with their eyes. For example, if one dog tries to take liberties, such as attempting to steal another dog's toy or bone, he may receive a long stare. Dogs use staring as a threat, and the would-be thief will recognize the danger and back down. Dogs also stare to tell other dogs who's boss, as Betty Fisher, a trainer and author of *So Your Dog's Not Lassie*, discovered when she introduced a new Newfoundland to her pack leader. "She turned her head, looked back over her shoulder, and stopped him dead in his tracks," Fisher says.

A stare helps in saving face as well. When he's playing, a dog may roll over onto his back—normally a submissive position—but he'll still make direct eye contact with the dog standing over him to show that he's not being cowardly.

Between people and dogs, eye contact doesn't usually mean a challenge or a threat. Dogs get used to humans looking directly at them, and they realize that our intentions are normally good. When dogs lock eyes with people, they're generally just fooling around or inviting them to play.

Blinking is another way dogs communicate with their eyes. When they meet for the first time, they'll sometimes give an exaggerated blink. This doesn't mean they're distracted or not interested. It's their way of saying that there's no problem or threat.

EYES AND EMOTIONS

You can tell a lot about what dogs are thinking and feeling by looking at their eyes. They use their eyes to express love and contentment, anxiety, and anger. Here's a guide to the most common expressions.

▶ Direct eye contact

Dogs who give you a keen and alert look are feeling happy and confident. The skin around their eyes will be smooth, with perhaps a small crease at the outside corners. This is how dogs look when they're greeting someone or inviting them to play, or when their owners have just given them something very desirable—like permission to snuggle up on the bed.

▼ Hard stare

Dogs stare when they've seen something that warrants closer attention, like an intruding cat. When they decide that further action is needed, they'll lower their heads a little and squint slightly. It's the same expression wolves use when they're watching their prey for weakness. Shepherds call this expression "the eye" and treasure it in herding dogs.

Dogs adopt a similar expression when they're feeling defensive, threatened, or aggressive. They'll raise their eyebrows, and the skin above their eyes will crinkle a little. Depending on what other emotions they're feeling, their foreheads may be furrowed. If they're aggressive, yet also feeling a bit fearful, their foreheads will be heavily furrowed. This is the expression some dogs show when, for example, the vacuum cleaner comes out of the closet. This look basically says, "I'm not sure if you're friend or foe."

◄ Averted gaze

Avoiding eye contact or looking away is how dogs try to keep the peace, says Steve Aiken, an animal behaviorist in Wichita, Kansas. It's how timid or submissive dogs say, "I don't want to cause any trouble. I know you're the boss." Dogs look this way when they meet other, more dominant dogs or when they sense they've done something to displease their owners.

Oblique stare

Sometimes, a stare isn't a sign of aggression. For example, dogs who are staring but trying hard not to show it, and whose eyes are almost closed, are planning something. Lying on the floor, supposedly snoozing, they're probably watching the cat but want to fool the cat into thinking they're asleep. Once the cat turns away, they'll probably pounce, hoping to entice the cat into a game.

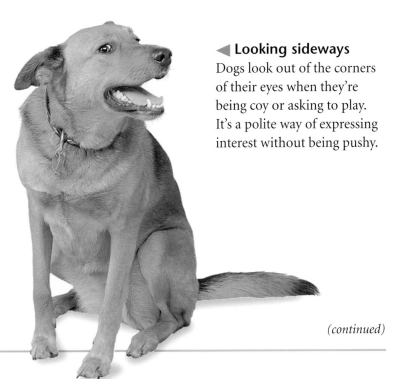

◄ Looking sideways

Dogs look out of the corners of their eyes when they're being coy or asking to play. It's a polite way of expressing interest without being pushy.

(continued)

EYES AND EMOTIONS—Continued

◀ Eyes opened wide

Wide eyes signify astonishment and surprise, and sometimes fear. A sudden noise can cause dogs to jump, turn around, and look wide-eyed at the source of the sound. Dogs who are frightened may open their eyes so wide that the whites show more than usual.

Blank stare

Blank stares don't need much interpretation—they mean bored dogs. If they're awake and their eyes are open but no one appears to be home, then they're in a bored-stiff trance. This can happen when dogs are forced to control themselves—for example, when their owners have told them to sit and stay while they're talking to a neighbor. Dogs may do as they're asked in such cases, but their blank stares express their boredom eloquently.

▶ Narrowed or half-closed eyes

Dogs who are happy and relaxed will narrow their eyes or half-close them. This is how dogs will look when they're enjoying something like a tummy rub or a long session of stroking from their owner. These half-closed eyes convey total bliss, and there's no misunderstanding that emotion.

CHAPTER FOURTEEN

EARS

Dogs use their ears for a lot more than hearing.
Their ears are mobile and expressive and they use them
to signal emotions to people and other dogs.

Dogs have excellent hearing, in part because their ears are wonderfully mobile. Controlled by about 15 different muscles, their ears swivel, twitch, rise up, and fall back. All of these movements allow dogs to detect faint sounds and pinpoint their direction. At the same time, their ear movements telegraph their moods and intentions, in the same way that our changing expressions and gestures tell others what we're feeling.

You can't gauge a dog's feelings by ear movements alone, any more than you can tell what people are thinking just by looking at their eyes, says Jacque Schultz, director of special projects for the Association for the Society and Preservation of Animals in New York City. You have to look at the ears in relation to other forms of body language, like the position of the tail or a dog's overall posture. This is especially true when you're dealing with dogs who have less-than-expressive ears, such as cropped or very long ones. "Dogs with cropped ears are limited in the amount of signals they can give," Schultz says. "They've been purposely made to look fierce and stoic so that they don't look to be showing pain or backing down in a fight."

All the positions of a dog's ears should be gauged in comparison to the way that a dog

PICK OF THE CROP

Breeds such as Doberman pinschers, boxers, Great Danes (below), and schnauzers have traditionally had cropped ears. These breeds naturally have hanging or folded ears, but cropping turns them into erect, pricked ears. This changes their look from gentle and placid to intent and aggressive, and that can change how people and other dogs perceive them. "Many crop-eared dogs unwittingly send the wrong message to other dogs," says D. Caroline Coile, Ph.D., a neuroscientist in Ochlocknee, Georgia. "They can't express a full range of emotions because they look perpetually aggressive and dominant."

normally carries his ears when he's relaxed, says Stanley Coren. Ph.D., professor of psychology at the University of British Columbia in Vancouver, Canada, and author of *The Intelligence of Dogs.* "Dogs with severely cropped ears will be harder to read," he says.

Some breeds are better at expressing certain emotions because of the shape of their ears. German shepherds, for example, have erect, triangular ears that make them look attentive and alert all the time, even when they're just casually looking around or dreaming about dinner. When they're focused and alert, their ears will become even more erect.

A basset hound, on the other hand, may be just as attentive as the German shepherd, but he can't convey the same degree of intensity. His heavy, pendulous ears simply aren't constructed for the task.

When you're watching dogs to see what their ears are saying, you need to take their ear types into consideration. You also need to look closely to interpret their ear language correctly. Some of the messages can be quite subtle, and positions that look very similar can mean different things, says D. Caroline Coile, a neuroscientist in with a special interest in canine sensory systems in Ochlocknee, Georgia.

BREED SPECIFIC

Some of the long-haired breeds, including cocker spaniels, poodles, Schnauzers and Lhasa apsos, grow hair in their ears. The combination of hair and ear wax sometimes makes an almost impregnable plug that blocks the ear canal. Hanging ears are also prone to health problems because of poor ventilation: Humidity builds up inside the ears and encourages the growth of fungi and bacteria. Hanging ears tend to trap grass seeds, as well. This is a perennial problem for cocker spaniels, who sometimes need surgery to remove the seeds. Floppy-eared dogs that enjoy playing in water, such as Labrador retrievers, golden retrievers, Chesapeake Bay retrievers, and Irish setters, are particularly vulnerable to ear problems, especially if care isn't taken to keep their ear canals clean and dry.

Prick-eared breeds have different health problems. Their ears seem to be a favorite target of biting insects, they're prone to sunburn, and they also run the risk of aural hematomas, a type of blood blister that causes the canine equivalent of "cauliflower ears".

Butterfly ears
Chinese crested dog

Semi-prick ears
Wire fox terrier

Judging Dogs by Their Ears

Even if you don't know a thing about reading ears, their shape and position can influence your perceptions of a dog's personality or temperament. Dogs with erect ears, such as corgis and Alaskan malamutes, always appear alert, intelligent, and assertive. Those with semi-erect ears, like collies, Shetland sheepdogs, and fox terriers, also look alert, but a little friendlier than those with fully erect ears. And dogs with hanging ears, such as basset hounds, beagles, Afghans, and Labradors, appear very friendly and placid. People are naturally attracted to these dogs because their hanging ears give them an appealingly docile, puppyish look.

It's unfortunate that very stylized ears can project confusing messages, at least to human eyes. Basset hounds, for example, usually have lively, sociable dispositions, but their floppy, long ears give them a mournful look. Cocker spaniels, on the other hand, have long, lavishly furred ears that make them look mellow, yet the reality is that they tend to be high-strung and excitable. And huskies have erect, triangular ears, which, along with their wolflike shape and coloring, don't convey their friendly, often docile natures.

POOCH ?? PUZZLER

Why do some dogs have floppy ears?

Most human ears are pretty much the same size and shape, but dogs have an amazing range of styles, from the neat, pricked ears of Samoyeds to the long, pendulous ones of bloodhounds. It wasn't always this way. Dogs are descended from wolves, and wolves don't have floppy ears. So what made some breeds' ears go from erect to floppy?

The answer is breeding. Tracking breeds such as beagles and bloodhounds were bred to track by scent alone, and their long ears help by dragging on the ground and stirring up air currents that make the scent molecules move around, says Anne Legge, a breeder of champion bloodhounds and judge of mantrailing trials in Winchester, Virginia.

Another reason for breeding dogs with floppy ears is that people simply like the docile, submissive look that long ears give. "Long ears set dogs' faces off in the same way that human hair does ours," says Jacque Schultz, director of special projects for the Association for the Society and Preservation of Animals in New York City. "They make their faces seem softer and more human-looking."

Hanging ears
Saluki

Folded ears
Whippet

Prick ears
Alaskan malamute

EAR POSITIONS

Although their ears come in a wondrous array of shapes and sizes, all dogs move them in similar ways to express what they're thinking and feeling. When you marry dogs' ear movements with what the rest of their bodies are telling you, you'll get a pretty clear picture of their state of mind.

▶ Neutral

Every dog, whether his ears are big, small, pricked, or floppy, has a neutral ear position that indicates he's relaxed and isn't thinking much about anything. The skin around the base of the ears will be smooth because he isn't making an effort to move the muscles. Dogs who are happy usually put their ears in the neutral position.

◀ Pricked up

Dogs who are stimulated by something they see or hear will prick their ears right up and point them in the direction of their interest. Dogs who are feeling aggressive will raise their ears, too. This is easiest to see in dogs that have prick ears, such as German shepherds. Dogs with folded or hanging ears, such as greyhounds or Labradors, aren't able to raise their ears as much, so the pricked-up response is harder to see. A clue to look for is creases around the base of the ear, which indicate that the muscles are active. "Watch the top of a dog's floppy ears," says John Hamil, D.V.M, a veterinarian and breeder of champion bloodhounds in Laguna Beach, California. "Floppy-eared dogs will pull their ears up toward the top of their heads when they're excited or interested in something."

The amount of tension in a dog's ears will tell you how strong his feelings are. There's more tension in an aggressive dog's ears than in those of a playfully alert dog.

◀ Pulled down and back

When a dog's brow and skull muscles are tight and tense, and his ears are pulled down and back, he's probably feeling frightened, anxious, or submissive. The more intense his feelings, the more extreme the ear position will be. Dogs also assume this position when they're wondering what's going to happen next or when they're play-fighting with other dogs. Putting the ears back seems to say, "This is just a game. I don't mean you any harm."

▶ Limp

Ears that droop like wet laundry are a dog's way of saying, "I'm bored stiff—not much action around here." Dogs with prick ears can't manage the full droop, but they'll let their ears sag sideways a bit. Those with naturally hanging ears will let them hang even lower.

◀ Multiple positions

Dogs are sometimes of two minds about things and this will show in the way they hold their ears. It's not unusual to see one ear pricked up while the other is partially pulled back. Or one ear may be folded while the other is flat against the skull. In some cases, the ears keep changing position as a dog's emotions change. You'll often see this when someone your dog doesn't know comes to the house. He's not sure whether to be excited or nervous, and his ears reflect his confusion.

CHAPTER FIFTEEN

TAIL

Dogs' tails are one of the most talkative parts of their bodies.
They can express happiness, aggression, stress,
and all the emotions in between.

Whether they're stately plumes, scruffy tangles, lively whips, or wagging stubs, dogs' tails are often moving and always talking. You can tell a lot about what dogs are feeling by the action of their tails. And the messages are often more complex than "Great, it's time to eat." Different wags show that dogs are nervous, shy, happy, or aggressive. Once you know what to look for, you'll know what they're feeling and even what they plan to do next.

When dogs are alone, they usually don't wag their tails, even when they're having a great time

UNNECESSARY SURGERY

Rottweilers, Dobermans, and boxers (right) are known for their stubby, assertive little tails, which zip back and forth like hyperactive metronomes. But these tails, common as they are, are artificially short, thanks to breed standards and a technique known as docking.

The various national breed clubs are responsible for defining the "ideal" look for different breeds. These looks are mainly achieved by selective breeding, but for some breeds, the natural tail doesn't meet the standard and is customarily docked, or cut short, a few days after birth.

Even though docking is common and many veterinarians don't see any harm in it, it does interfere with a dog's ability to communicate, says Barbara Simpson, Ph.D., a veterinary behaviorist in Southern Pines, North Carolina.

"He doesn't have as many components to let him express what he's feeling, but if the other dogs are well-socialized, they can pick up enough information from the other signals that dogs with docked tails send."

BREED SPECIFIC

Most dogs have tails that are the same color as the rest of their coat. But some dogs, including beagles, basset hounds, and Tibetan terriers, have tails of a different color, especially at the tip. This allows their tails to act as attention-getting flags, making it much easier for them to signal their intentions to other dogs.

excavating the garden or barking at birds that are flying overhead. The reason for this is that tail-wagging is mainly used for social communication, much as people trade small talk at office parties. Once a dog gets around people or other dogs, the tail really goes into action.

How fast and vigorously it moves depends on the breed and the dog's personality. Some dogs, such as Cavalier King Charles spaniels, tend to wag wildly at the slightest provocation. Other breeds, such as Rottweilers, don't wag anywhere near as much.

Among all breeds, a slight wag, when just the end of the tail moves, is considered a casual greeting. The happier and more excited dogs get, the more vigorously they wag. Tails that are stiff and not wagging are a signal that dogs are feeling defensive, protective, or aggressive.

"One trick that a dog doesn't need to learn is how to wag his tail," writes Marjorie Garber, author of *Dog Love*. "A wagging tail is the spontaneous sign of joyful recognition, and dog owners usually respond to it with a joyful recognition of their own. For the dog wears his heart on his tail."

Different Tails, Different Tales

Not every dog is adept in tail-speak. Just as some people are less articulate than others, some dogs don't communicate very well with their tails. This has less to do with ability than genetics: Some breeds have tails that are less mobile than others. Others have tails that are held close to their rumps. No matter how much they try to communicate, their tails won't cooperate.

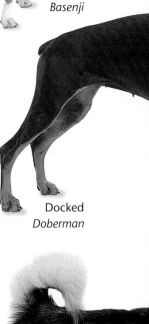

Tightly curled
Basenji

Docked
Doberman

Bushy
Alaskan malamute

This can be a real problem for dogs like French bulldogs, basenjis, and pugs, whose tails are small and tightly curled. They tend to rely on other types of body language when they need to express their emotions, says Shirley Thomas, an American Kennel Club judge and champion pug breeder in Flushing, New York, and author of *The New Pug*. When they're happy, they wiggle their bodies back and forth and shake their tails from side to side.

"They also use their heads a lot. They'll wrinkle their foreheads when they're curious, and they can move their ears into many different positions," she says.

Short and upright
*West Highland
white terrier*

**High and
stiff**
Airedale

Between legs
Greyhound

Australian shepherds are born with very short tails, or, in some cases, with no tails at all. Boxers, schnauzers, Rottweilers, and Doberman pinschers customarily have their tails docked, or cut short. These dogs use their stubby tails as much as they can, but their ability to express themselves is quite restricted.

Some tails, on the other hand, are made for communication because they're easy to see. Dogs with long, bushy, eye-catching tails, such as German shepherds, Samoyeds, and Siberian huskies, don't have any trouble expressing their emotions. Not only do their tails move freely, but the luxuriant masses of hair can be made to rise at a moment's notice, giving them charisma and an air of authority.

Scottish terriers and West Highland white terriers are between these two extremes. While their tails are quite short, and short-haired, they're still very expressive because what they lack in size they make up for in mobility and upright positioning, says Mary Warzecha, a columnist for the *American Kennel Club Gazette* in Windsor, Connecticut.

While a hairy tail can make it easier to communicate by exaggerating dogs' normal tail movements, it can also be a problem for dogs with very short tails, like Old English sheepdogs. Their thick, hairy coats can cover their tails like a comforter. No matter how much they move their tails, the movements may be invisible. To compensate, these dogs will often move their entire rumps back and forth.

Judging Dogs by Their Tails

Dogs are rarely standoffish and they're never prejudiced. A German shepherd won't make judgments about a Labrador, and a poodle is perfectly happy playing with a golden retriever. People, on the other hand, are quick to form judgments not only about each other but also about dogs. And to a large extent these judgments are shaped by a dog's tail.

Consider Welsh terriers. They have wildly wagging, jaunty tails that ride high on the rump, and they make people smile just to see them. Great Danes, on the other hand, have tails that attach to the body lower on the rump. To human eyes, this can make them seem a little moody or aloof. No matter how happy or friendly they actually are, their low-set tails don't seem quite as welcoming as the high-flying tails of some other dogs.

Different breeds carry their tails in different positions as well. Fox terriers and Airedales, for example, naturally carry their tails high and rather stiffly. This can make them look assertive or even aggressive—not only to people but also to other dogs. Vizslas and golden retrievers carry their tails in a more relaxed fashion, and

this makes them look mellow and unthreatening. Greyhounds, whippets, borzois, and Afghan hounds usually carry their tails between their legs. People often think they're timid, frightened, or unhappy, but they're not. It's just how their tails are.

Tails and Scent Communication

Dogs' tails have one other vital role in communicating: Every time a dog moves his tail, it acts like a fan and spreads his natural *eau de dog* around him, just as a woman walking through a crowd may leave a lingering aroma of perfume.

Dogs use their sense of smell much more than people do, and one odor that always gets their attention comes from the anal glands, two sacs under the tail that contain an odoriferous liquid that's as unique among dogs as fingerprints are among people. By smelling this scent, dogs can determine many interesting facts, such as each other's sex, age, and status, says Deena Case-Pall, Ph.D., a psychologist and animal behaviorist in Camarillo, California.

POOCH PUZZLER

Why do dogs chase their tails?

Dogs look like they're having a great time when they're spinning in circles and trying to catch their tails. But sometimes it's not any fun at all. "They may have an irritation on their backs, an itchy bottom, or a flea allergy," says Dick Schumacher, D.V.M., a veterinarian and executive director of the California Veterinary Medical Association in Davis, California.

If a trip to the veterinarian doesn't reveal any problems, and your dog is still chasing his rear end, then he really is doing it for fun. "Some dogs just see their tails and want to know all about them," says Steve Aiken, an animal behaviorist in Wichita, Kansas.

While dogs with long tails tend to chase them more often than do those with very short tails, it's not a very common activity. "And some dogs never chase their tails at all," says Dr. Schumacher.

It's the dog equivalent of reading someone's driver's license and finding out all their pertinent information," she says. From the details they glean, dogs can tell whether to be respectful or disdainful, lustful or indifferent.

Every time a dog wags his tail, the muscles around his anus contract, pressing on the glands and releasing the scent. A dominant dog who carries his tail high will release much more scent

Tail-wagging helps distribute a dog's unique odor so others can learn more about him.

89

than a submissive dog who holds his tail lower. And the wagging of his tail, of course, helps to distribute the scent.

One of the reasons that nervous, frightened, or submissive dogs hold their tails between their legs is to prevent other dogs from sniffing them. It's their way of trying to fade into the background and not draw attention to themselves.

Tails in Action

When dogs aren't communicating with their tails, they can find plenty of other useful things to do with them. For a start, the tail is a vital part of a dog's balance system. Some breeds, like Afghans, Irish wolfhounds, and greyhounds, were bred to chase fast-moving prey. Their tails are thin and very long in proportion to the rest of them. They can run at great speeds, and they use their tails as a counterbalance when turning. Their long tails give them agility and the ability to turn quickly in response to the movements of their prey, says Lou Gerrero, a breeder of champion Afghans and an American Kennel Club judge in Simi Valley, California. "These dogs' tails are long, tapered, and low-set, and when

When greyhounds run, they use their long, thin tails as rudders to help them turn quickly.

combined with their sloping rumps, there's a powerful rudder effect."

Dogs also use their tails as rudders when they're swimming. Chesapeake Bay retrievers and Labrador retrievers have tails that are thick and strong, which helps them move easily through the water. Their tails are also very flexible and this helps them make quick turns in the water, explains Janet Horn, a breeder of champion Chesapeake Bay retrievers in Frenchtown, New Jersey.

Other dogs use their tails as convenient form of insulation. Nordic breeds such as Siberian huskies, Samoyeds, Alaskan malamutes, and keeshonds have brushy or plumed tails with long, dense fur. When they're lying down, they can pull their tails over their faces to keep out the cold, says Vicky Jones, a breeder of Alaskan malamutes in Sharpsburg, Georgia.

"These dogs also use their tails to help them move a bit faster when they're pulling a sled across ice because their tails act like a rudder," Jones says.

Tail Positions and Movements

You can tell a lot about dogs by the ways they move their tails. Tail-wagging is just part of their repertoire. The position of the tail is also significant. By looking at the position and movement of dogs' tails, you can get a pretty good idea of what they're trying to say.

▶ Sweeping from side to side

Dogs often wag their tails in broad sweeps when they're playing or anticipating something good, like food. But they also use this wag when they're throwing their weight around or getting ready to launch an attack, says Petra Horn, a trainer in Mira Mesa, California. The only way to know the difference is to look at other cues, such as the way they're standing, to tell what their intentions are.

◀ High and wagging

Dogs are always in good moods when their tails are held high and are wagging back and forth. The speed of the wag will increase dramatically when they get a good response from whomever they're hoping to engage in play.

(continued)

TAIL POSITIONS AND MOVEMENTS—CONTINUED

◀ Horizontal

You can tell a dog is interested in something when his tail is horizontal to the ground. This signal is only evident in dogs with long tails, of course. Those with short or docked tails will express the same message by holding the tail slightly higher than usual, says Kathy Marmack, a supervisor of animal training at the San Diego Zoo in California.

▶ Tucked

Submissive, anxious, or frightened dogs invariably tuck their tails between their legs. The farther a dog tucks his tail, the stronger his feelings. A dog who's extremely frightened will tuck his tail so much that it may reach all the way to his stomach. Even when the tail is tucked, however, the tip will wag a bit, which displays his stress.

A tucked tail isn't always a sad sight. It's normal for puppies, for example, to tuck their tails when they're greeting adult dogs. It's their way of showing respectful submission. Once the adult accepts a young dog's greeting, the tail will uncoil and start moving more naturally again.

▶ High and rigid

When a dog's tail goes from being horizontal to upright and rigid, you can be pretty sure that an interesting situation has turned into a potentially challenging or threatening one, says Janice DeMello, an obedience trainer in Somis, California. Dogs who are trying to assert their authority will usually raise their tails slightly above the horizontal. To make themselves appear even stronger and more dominant, they'll raise the tail even more and wag it slightly back and forth. You can tell a dog is truly annoyed or angry when the tail goes almost rigid. If anger gives way to actual aggression, the tail will go higher still and it

won't move at all. However, the hair will bristle and rise on end. This is how dogs make themselves appear bigger than they really are. Hair on the shoulders and back, called the hackles, will start to bristle, too.

▶ Low and moving slightly

While dogs experiencing anger or other "high" emotions will raise their tails, those feeling a little low will make them droop. A tail held below horizontal and wagging very slightly means a lowering of spirits. Such a dog is slightly worried or a bit insecure. Or he may be feeling a little sick.

CHAPTER SIXTEEN

HOW TO PREVENT CONFUSION

Dogs are often mystified by our body language and tone of voice.
Understanding what they do respond to makes it
easier for us to send the right messages in the right way.

Even though dogs can recognize and understand some human words and body language, most of the ways we behave and communicate seem a little foreign to them. They try to understand what they see and hear by translating human behavior into canine terms, and that's when confusion sets in.

People move their hands a lot when they get excited, for example, and dogs have seen us do it a hundred times. They know from our energy and expressions that we're happy, and yet they can't help suspecting that we're angry because in the animal world, quick, exuberant movements usually mean aggression or danger rather than fun and happiness.

Confusion is also an issue when we tell dogs to do things and they don't do them. Maybe you yell at a dog to stop barking, and he keeps barking. Or you say "heel," and your dog forges ahead. It often seems as though the more insistent people get, the worse their dogs behave, and so frustration levels rise. "People think that their dogs are stubborn, but there's no such thing as a stubborn dog, just a dog who's been given confusing signals," says Chuck Tompkins, an animal behaviorist and vice

Dogs respond best when our words and body language convey the same message. This miniature poodle is ignoring the command to come because she interprets her owner's exuberance as anger.

president of animal training at Sea World International in Orlando, Florida.

When you consider that dogs and people are different species with entirely different ways of communicating and viewing the world, it makes sense that a certain amount of confusion is unavoidable. Dogs don't have the capacity to understand humans, but we do have the capacity to understand them. Once you understand how dogs perceive you—your tone of voice, your body language, and the many ways in which you express yourself—the communication barriers become less insurmountable.

Vocal Barriers

People's speaking voices can throw dogs into a quandary. They're familiar with the range and volume of their owners' voices, of course, but voices that they don't know can be confusing. Dogs don't listen to words that much, but they are attentive to such things as tone and laughter, and they're very good at comparing voices with body language. That's why people can be saying one thing while their dogs are hearing something entirely different.

Tone of voice. Dogs are very sensitive to the tone of people's voices. In their world, young or submissive dogs are the ones with high-pitched barks or yelps, while more dominant dogs are the ones most likely to give a low growl.

It's not uncommon for dogs to get slightly nervous around men with deep voices because they associate that pitch with authority—or, in some cases, with the reprimands their mothers gave them when they were young. The men, of course, don't understand any of this, or why they're getting such a negative reaction.

People don't have to disguise their voices to communicate with dogs, but raising the pitch a little can help. To a dog's ears a higher voice sounds less threatening and happier. Trainers often recommend using an energetic, slightly high-pitched tone with all dogs, not just those who get nervous around deep voices, because it can help dogs respond with more enthusiasm.

While low-pitched voices cause the most confusion for dogs, high-pitched voices cause problems of their own, especially when they're used for discipline. Suppose you're leash-training your dog, and he's forging head, zig-zagging across your path and generally doing just about everything except heeling. If you have a high voice and give a reprimand—and people's voices usually get higher when they're tense—your dog may act as he would with a young or subservient dog and just ignore you.

Whether your voice is naturally high or low, it's worth lowering it a notch when giving reprimands. Even if you don't sound angry, the deep, gruff tone will spark your dog's memories of early authority figures, and he'll be more likely to do as you tell him.

Words and actions. Dogs are experts at reading all kinds of body language, which means that they can quickly tell when your

This toy poodle is very sensitive to his owner's tone of voice. Men with deep voices often get better results when they raise the pitch while praising their dogs.

words or tone of voice aren't telling the whole story. This often happens in vets' offices, where anxious owners try to soothe nervous dogs by telling them that everything's okay. The dogs know perfectly well that everything's not okay, and their owners' attempts to give comfort may have the opposite effect. It's as though the dogs are thinking, "Things must be pretty bad if she's going to lie like that."

Things get even worse when dogs start growling because they're scared. It's natural to want to reassure a frightened dog, but doing so will probably increase his tension because he'll interpret soothing words as support for what he's doing, says Moira Cornell, an obedience trainer in Canoga Park, California. This type of confusion can be a problem because your dog simply won't understand that what he's doing isn't appropriate, she explains.

A better approach is to tell your dog in no uncertain terms to cut it out, she advises. He'll respect the firmness in your voice, and the clarity of the message will take some of the pressure off him. He'll realize that you're in charge and will be able to handle things from then on.

Laughter. It takes almost superhuman willpower not to laugh when dogs are acting silly or when they're trying to do something serious but wind up looking silly anyway. It's important to refrain from laughing when dogs have done something wrong, because dogs interpret laughter as a happy sound that means they have your full approval. Laughing when they do something wrong makes them think you approve—and to keep getting your approval in the future, they're sure to do the same thing wrong again.

Body Language Barriers

When dogs want to learn more about other dogs, they focus on posture. From a distance, a dog can figure out what another dog is thinking by looking at how he holds his body and tail. An alert pose means that he's attentive. When he's standing stiffly, with his tail straight out and wagging rhythmically, it means that he's cautious and on guard.

Dog-to-dog messages are pretty clear-cut because both dogs are speaking the same language. But dogs are in foreign territory when they try to decipher human body language, especially because our bodies sometimes contradict our voices or expressions.

It's important when dealing with dogs to be aware of your body language and to make sure that it's communicating the same thing as your voice. Your voice and body language are likely to be at odds when you're cross with your dog but are trying not to show it. No matter what you're saying, your dog will see that your face, arms, and shoulders are stiff. They're all signs that you're on edge, and he'll be confused because you haven't sent him a clear message about what you're feeling. Your voice may be saying that everything's fine, but if your body is saying that it's not, your dog won't know which signal he's supposed to believe.

The trick is to keep your posture as relaxed as you can when you're interacting with your dog, says Cornell. If your shoulders and arms are rigid and your expression stern, your dog will sense that you're angry because he pays more attention to your body than to the words that you say.

ACTING THE PART

Dogs in the movies look natural, but what's on the screen represents hours of training. Scripts often call for dogs to do things that are contrary to their natural behavior. It's up to a trainer to ensure that the dogs understand exactly what they're supposed to do.

To successfully train a dog to "act," trainers must have a dog's total attention no matter what comes up, says Mary Kay Snyder, who trained the Dalmatian puppies in the movie *101 Dalmatians.* Most trainers use a clicker to let dogs know that a treat is coming when they do their jobs correctly.

"An actor dog is conditioned to pay attention and perform the command. Then he expects to hear the clicker go off. Once the scene is over, the dog is rewarded with a treat," says Snyder.

Since dogs in the movies are often shown running, they have to learn to run on a treadmill. It's the only way to film scenes that are shot in a studio.

"It's a pretty boring activity, yet we want a dog to look excited and not get confused," Snyder says. "I condition him to watch me running in front of him."

Dog actors also have to learn to run in one direction, then suddenly stop and run the other way. "With this trick we have someone call a dog to come one way, then his trainer calls him from the other direction," Snyder says.

It often takes three or four months to train dogs for film sequences. A vital part of the preparation is to take the dogs to a variety of places before they put a paw on the set. "I want to accustom them to hearing different sounds and meeting different people so that nothing surprises or confuses them," Snyder says. This will help them act calmly around the loud noises, strange people, and large equipment found in a movie studio or on location. They also have to be comfortable on set with creatures they don't see every day, such as chickens or pigs.

Dog actors, like this miniature schnauzer, are trained to focus intently on their trainers and to stay calm in all sorts of unusual situations.

Mental Barriers

It's normal for us to interpret dogs' behavior in human terms, but our judgments usually aren't very accurate. Dogs have rich emotional lives, but their emotions aren't the same as ours. People often swear that their dogs look guilty when they've done something wrong. But dogs don't feel guilt—at least, not in the same way we do. That means that when you come home and find the trash on the floor and your dog cowering in the corner, you can't assume that he knows he did something wrong. In all likelihood he's responding to the look on your face, and he knows it doesn't look good. As for the trash at his feet, he's probably forgotten it was his doing in the first place.

Staffordshire bull terriers often have a dominant streak. Indulging them with rough play, which they adore, will only reinforce their dominant tendencies.

More confusion may arise when you start cleaning up the mess. You're in a bad mood and angry, and you get even angrier when your dog, rather than looking abashed, starts rooting around in the trash for extra tidbits. He's not being disrespectful, says Jayme Evans, a dog trainer and founder of Canine College in Middleburg, Virginia. In his mind, since you're touching the mess, it must be okay for him to touch it, too. He's just following the leader, which is what dogs do naturally.

The important thing is to always make your reaction match the situation. Your dog needs to be able to make a logical connection between what he did and your response if he's to understand what you really mean. He may not like being corrected, but at least he'll see that as a logical response. But starting to scold your dog, then suddenly relenting and indulgently giving his ears a scratch will seem inconsistent and illogical—and that will leave him baffled and confused.

Mistaking who's in charge. Dogs like to know who's in charge, and mostly they're very happy for their owners to take on that role. But sometimes people give the wrong message, making dogs think the role has passed to them. And that can cause all sorts of problems.

Questions of leadership often occur during play. When dogs play with one another, the action is rough-and-tumble. They're fast and athletic, and they use every part of their bodies to prove they're rougher and tougher than their opponents. The goal of their games is often to see who backs down first. It's all in fun, but underneath the fun is a genuine contest for control and dominance.

The same motivations can underlie their play with humans. People who play roughly with their dogs by wrestling or pulling on a rope are creating a situation in which dogs feel they have to win. This usually isn't a problem because whether dogs win or lose, they had a great time. But some dogs are naturally more dominant than others, and there's no way they'll willingly lose without putting up a fight.

"With dogs that have a tendency to be aggressive, it's not a good idea to wrestle or play tug games," says Evans. If they're losing, they may get increasingly rough until they think they are winning. If you deliberately let them win, they'll come away feeling as though they have the upper hand. This can cause all kinds of problems, not just during play but also during the rest of your time together.

Even with dogs that aren't aggressive, rough-and-tumble romping can get out of hand quickly. Dogs play with people the same way they play with dogs—by play-biting. But they don't take into account that while dogs have protective layers of fur and loose skin that can withstand a certain amount of playful mauling, people don't. That means that people can't take the same level of rough stuff that another dog can—so an owner who's having fun one minute can be in pain and angry the next. The result is canine confusion.

Appearance Barriers

Dogs watch people much more closely than we ever watch them. Should our facial expressions not match the other signals that we're giving, dogs get confused. When you're trying to act

This woman's upbeat tone of voice, happy facial expression, and relaxed posture are all sending the same message, so her Belgian shepherd knows for sure that she's happy with him.

stern, for example, but your eyes are twinkling or your mouth is curving into a smile, dogs aren't sure which to believe—your stern voice or your happy facial expression.

Likewise, if you use a serious voice to tell your dog to stay but a few seconds later give him a wink, he'll think that you're giving him permission to get up and move around.

Putting on a happy face does come in handy when you want to congratulate a dog for following orders. But don't try to fool dogs with "false" expressions, and try not to mix the signals you're giving. Dogs only feel secure when they know what you're feeling; mixed signals make them nervous and uncertain.

PART FOUR

FAILURE TO COMMUNICATE

Many communication problems begin when a dog is
unsure of who's the boss. To establish leadership and avoid
communication breakdowns, you need to use your body language,
facial expressions, and voice effectively. At the same time,
you need to read your dog's signals correctly.

CHAPTER SEVENTEEN

WHO'S IN CHARGE?

Every dog will be happier if he knows who's in charge.
By letting your dog know you're the boss, you'll
make life easier for both of you.

Children learn from their parents and teachers to share their toys, to play fair, and, above all, not to be bossy. And if they don't learn from their parents, they quickly learn on the playground that other children don't like being bossed around.

Dogs see things differently. They love to be bossed around. In fact, dogs *need* to be bossed around, especially by the people in their lives.

Dogs are pack animals. What this means is that when they lived in the wild they lived in highly structured societies. They relied on a leader in order to survive. Dogs today don't have the same survival imperatives, but the old instincts remain. Dogs think of their human family as their pack, and they look to their owner to be the leader of the pack.

"Dogs feel more secure when they know who's the leader," says Sandy Myers, director of Narnia Pet Training in Naperville, Illinois. "Their packs are linear, with one member at the top. If we humans don't take on that role, our dogs will take it."

Most dogs don't want to be the leader. They'd much rather let you call the shots. But if you have a live-and-let-live philosophy, they'll often get uneasy because they're not sure where to turn for leadership. So they step in, however reluctantly, to fill the void.

When a dog does attempt to become the family's leader, problems can follow. Rather than taking orders from you, he'll become increasingly dominant, says Yody Blass, an animal behaviorist and director of Companion Animal Behavior in Ashburn, Virginia. "He may start growling, nipping, or even biting whenever he feels the need," Blass says.

It's important to teach your puppy early in life to respect your leadership and your rules.

Once a dog starts taking charge, he may be reluctant to give up his new-found power. This means he'll keep biting and growling and pushing you around until someone—it could be you or a member of your family—finally steps in to take control.

That's why you need to establish your authority, to make sure that your dog realizes that you're in charge, not him. "You need to be a benevolent leader," says Robin Kovary, director of the American Dog Trainers Network in New York City. "A good leader is never abusive. Dominance doesn't mean being harsh."

How to Lead Your Dog

Leadership comes from clear communication and consistency. Dogs can't reason, second-guess you, or ask questions when they're confused, so you need to make it absolutely clear what you want from them. And because they don't appreciate a wishy-washy leader, you need to lay—and then stick to—a few firm ground rules. That way, they'll know what's expected of them and will respond better. Here are some tips on becoming and staying your dog's most-trusted leader.

Be consistent. When your dog gets different messages from different people, he'll become confused. Worse, he may decide that since there are two (or more) sets of rules, any rules that come from humans are made to be challenged. "It's important to develop reasonable guidelines for your dog, and then make sure that everyone in your family agrees to them," says Kovary. For example, if you don't want your dog jumping on the sofa or beds, the whole family has to go

When he hears the command "off!" given consistently and clearly, this kelpie-Labrador cross will soon learn not to jump on people.

along with this—and that means keeping him off the tables and chairs, as well.

It's also important to enforce your rules consistently. When you boot your dog off the sofa on Monday, but let him hop up on Tuesday, he'll soon learn to not take your rules seriously.

Take a firm stand. "Never allow or encourage aggressive or bratty behavior in a puppy," says Kovary. It's cute when puppies mouth your hands or jump on you while you're playing. But that behavior won't be so cute once your puppy becomes a full-grown dog.

Reinforce good behavior. Parents encourage their children to do the right thing by rewarding them for good behavior. Dogs respond to compliments, too. In fact, your dog will learn what you want him to learn much more quickly when he gets positive reinforcement—a word of praise when he sits right away, for example, or a treat when he comes running when you call.

Instill a work ethic. Some dogs are never required to do anything. They come when they want, lie where it pleases them, and feel free to ignore you when it suits their fancy. Not surprisingly, these are usually dogs with attitude problems. To keep your dog honest, it's always a good idea to make him work for some of his rewards. That way your dog will quickly learn that the way to happiness comes through pleasing you, his leader.

For example, have your dog sit at the front door before you let him walk out. Tell him to sit and wait while you place his food bowl in front of him. Make him sit or lie down before being petted, or before greeting you or any visitors. And always reward his obedience with praise, a pat, or a treat. Your dog will soon learn that service and obedience are the keys to making both of you happy.

Defusing Dominance

Most dogs are happy to have a human leader. Sometimes, though, a dog will challenge you for leadership. He may do this with subtle signals—

MAKING THE INTRODUCTION

Dogs are territorial, so they get nervous when others invade their turf. That's why trainers recommend introducing dogs away from home, when they don't have territory to defend.

"Always introduce two dogs on neutral ground, such as in a park," says Wendy Volhard, a dog trainer in Phoenix, New York. "You don't want to put your dog in a position of having to defend his territory." Once the dogs have been properly introduced, it's fine to take them both home, but you'll still need to respect the resident dog's status, Volhard says. That means letting the "main" dog through the door first when you arrive home. He'll probably turn around and look at the newcomer. Then, in some subtle way, he'll let him know that it's okay to follow. And once they're friends, you won't have to worry about conflicts later on.

---

like lying on your feet and refusing to move when you try to stand up—or by actually acting aggressive. When this happens, you need to take serious steps to manage him. The key is to let him know that you're the one in charge, but without provoking a confrontation. This is one situation in which you don't want to move too fast because once a dog has started asserting his dominance, he'll perceive any opposition as a challenge and will be more likely to stand his ground. Your goal is to gradually assert your leadership while reducing your dog's tendency towards aggressiveness.

Give him less protein. Many dogs get too much protein in their diets. Extra protein means extra energy—and in dogs that have strong, dominant personalities, extra energy can lead to further contests of wills. Look for dog food with protein levels of under 20 percent, says Ilana Reisner, D.V.M., a veterinarian and animal behaviorist at Cornell University in Ithaca, New York.

Get him moving. Exercise siphons off a dog's excess energy, which in turn can dampen his desire to be boss. It also releases endorphins, calming chemicals in the brain that can help put your dog in a better mood. Try to get him walking, jogging, or doing other strenuous exercise for at least 20 minutes a day. Large dogs or dogs that are unusually active, like Border collies, can use a lot more.

Avoid confrontations. There are two situations that often trigger confrontations from dogs with dominant tendencies. The first is competition over a prized object. Until your dog has started to learn his proper place in the family, don't take away his toys or anything else that he considers to be his. (At least, avoid doing it when he's looking; it's fine to spirit away "trouble" objects when he's not around.) The second main cause of confrontations is a reac-

This Yorkshire terrier has learned to sit and wait for permission before eating his dinner.

tion to a perceived threat. Dominant dogs may react badly to being surprised, so try not to disturb him when he's resting, or come up suddenly from behind.

Even though it's your job as the leader to call the shots, there's nothing wrong with cutting your dog some slack while you're teaching him to be subordinate. A face-to-face confrontation will only stiffen his resolve, whereas making gradual adjustments in your relationship is more likely to lead to lasting changes.

Practice obedience commands. This is a good way to reinforce your leadership and teach your dog to respect it. You don't need to be a master trainer or to spend hours every day having formal, parade-ground drill sessions. The idea is to get your dog used to following simple commands—such as sit, down, stay, or come—and to repeat the lessons twice a day for 5 to 10 minutes. Once your dog is following your commands during these training sessions, he'll be more likely to follow them the rest of the time. You can use these commands to make him earn whatever it is that he wants, whether it's toys, treats, or time with you.

Set the pace. Being a leader is a full-time job. Even when you and your dog are playing, you need to be the

105

These German shepherds follow their owner's lead and let her set the pace in the games that they play.

best to avoid rough games, like wrestling and tug-of-war. These activities encourage aggression by pitting your dog against you. When a naturally dominant dog wins such a game, he'll think he's one step closer to knocking you off the leader's rung.

Outsmart him. No matter how dominant your dog has been acting, you have a tremendous advantage: You're a lot smarter than he is. This means you don't always have to resort to confrontation—sometimes a little sneakiness will do the trick. Suppose, for example, your dog makes off with something he's not supposed to, like your shoe, and then acts aggressive when you try to get it back. You don't have to force the issue. Instead, offer him something he wants more, like a favorite toy or treat. Then when your dog drops your shoe, discreetly kick it away from him and out of sight. Then you can retrieve it later.

Leading a Multi-Dog Household

The best relationships between people and dogs are those in which the people are the leaders and the dogs know it. This is especially true in a multi-dog household.

In any group of dogs, no matter how large or small, there's a very strict order. There's one dog who's the leader, and every other dog knows his place in the group and what's expected of him. Usually, the individual dogs will sort out the

one in charge. This means that you, not he, decide when playtime starts and when it stops. You decide whether he should play vigorously or whether he should take it easy. And when you're done playing, simply take your ball and go home. He'll learn to follow your lead instead of trying to make you follow his.

You should also be the one who decides which games to play. The best games are those in which you give commands and so reinforce your leadership. When you're throwing a ball, for example, you call the shots by making your dog drop the ball every time he retrieves it. It's

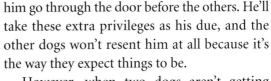

hierarchy on their own without help from you. But owners sometimes make it harder for dogs to work things out because they try to make everything equal between their dogs. "This causes stress among the dogs, and that results in a battle for leadership," says Myers. "Each dog has his place and if we disrupt that, the lead dog will try to set things right. There's no equality in a group of dogs."

You can help to keep things stable in a multi-dog household by working out which is the lead dog and then respecting his rank. "To see who the lead dog is, figure out what each dog values," suggests Myers. "It's different for each dog—say, petting for one dog, food for another. Then watch to see which dog will leave his most valued item when the other approaches. Usually, the one that doesn't move away is the leader."

Once you figure out which dog is the canine leader, make sure you respect the pecking order. This means paying attention to the lead dog first in all things. For example, feed him before the other dogs, greet him first when you get home, and let

This miniature schnauzer is the top dog in the family, so he gets fed first. The toy poodle, as his follower, eats a little later.

him go through the door before the others. He'll take these extra privileges as his due, and the other dogs won't resent him at all because it's the way they expect things to be.

However, when two dogs aren't getting along, you'll need to step in. Lindsley Cross of Carmichael, California, learned this first-hand when she brought home Rosie, a six-month-old terrier-pointer mix. Cross's other dog, a two-year-old kelpie mix named B. G., was happy to share Cross with the newcomer. Rosie, however, hated it when B. G. got any attention. She would push Cross away whenever she tried to pet the older dog. Rosie also started stealing B. G.'s rest spots and playing roughly with her, sometimes making her yelp with pain.

B. G. never stood up to Rosie, and Cross didn't intervene, so the situation didn't improve. After five months of bullying and pushy behavior, Cross had had enough, and asked experienced dog owners for advice. They told her to deep-six her laissez-faire approach and to stop Rosie's rough play the minute it starts—by telling Rosie "no," for example, and by holding her away from B. G. when she started muscling in.

And that's all it took. Rosie is still a little pushy, Cross says, but she's learned she can't get away with being too aggressive. In addition, B. G. naturally got more assertive once Cross started acting as a backup. The dogs will always compete, but now it's more of a friendly contest than a battle for control.

CHAPTER EIGHTEEN

SENDING MIXED MESSAGES

What dogs hear is not always what people say.
Knowing how such misunderstandings occur is one step toward
communicating more clearly with our dogs.

We spend a lot of time with our dogs and get to know them pretty well. But it's worth remembering that we're a completely different species, with very different ways of communicating. That's why, despite our best intentions, we occasionally send mixed signals, telling our dogs one thing when what we mean is something else entirely.

Suppose your dog is merrily barking away in the backyard. If you're like most people, you'll eventually respond by sticking your head out the door and yelling "quiet"—at which point your dog starts barking even more loudly. This is a classic case of mixed signals. You thought your message was perfectly clear. But your dog interpreted your yelling differently. "Great," she

Volume doesn't mean the same thing to dogs as it does to people. That's why yelling at your dog to stop barking can sometimes encourage her to bark more.

probably thought. "She's barking too, and now we can do it together."

These sorts of misunderstandings don't have to happen. Once you understand how your dog thinks, you'll discover how to communicate in ways that she can clearly understand.

Differences in Body Language

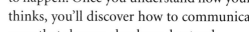

People and dogs often get their wires crossed because they have different interpretations of body language. Hand movements, posture, and even facial expressions have entirely different meanings for people and dogs. Take a smile. Among humans it's a sign of friendship and pleasure. But dogs mostly "smile" when they're acting aggressively—and they assume that others do it for the same reason, says Sandy Myers, director of Narnia Pet Training in Naperville, Illinois. So your good-hearted greeting, meant to put a dog at ease, may get a cool reception.

This doesn't mean you should greet your dog with a frozen face. Dogs understand their owners better than we often think, and they learn to read human signals even when they're different from their own. But when you're dealing with an unfamiliar dog on the street or in someone's home, you might want to save the smile for later, when the dog has a better sense of who you are and feels comfortable with you.

The same goes for eye contact. Among people it's a sign of courtesy and confidence. We respect people who look us in the eye. Those who avoid eye contact, on the other hand, often appear distracted or even shifty. But among dogs, the opposite is true. Direct eye contact is often perceived as a challenge or a sign of aggression. A dog who stares directly at another dog is saying, "I want to be in charge here." The second dog, if she's a peaceful sort, will avert her eyes. Or, if she's not feeling peaceable, she'll stare right back, which means she's not backing down and is ready for trouble.

Dogs can certainly learn that eye contact from humans is perfectly acceptable, but this level of understanding takes time. When you're greeting a dog you don't know very well, the last thing you want is to unintentionally challenge her. At the very least, she'll have a hard time trusting you; at worst, you could get bitten. A better way to greet dogs is to look away, says Robin Kovary, director of the American Dog Trainers Network in New York City. This gives them a chance to approach and give you a sniff without feeling threatened. Once you get to know each other, it's fine to make eye contact because they'll recognize that humans don't know all the rules and will make allowances for this type of social faux pas.

Posture is another way in which we occasionally send the wrong signals. People move their hands a lot when they talk, or they stand tall and open their arms in an embracing gesture. From a dog's point of view, these expansive gestures and quick hand movements

This Irish wolfhound prefers being greeted with indirect eye contact and slow, calm movements.

can be unnerving because that's simply not how dogs greet each other. They're much less direct: They sidle up to strangers, moving slowly so as not to arouse suspicion. This is why dogs often shy away when someone approaches too quickly or with a lot of energy. Your hearty good-will and glad-to-see-you exuberance can seem vaguely threatening, at least until they get to know you better.

Personal Space

When it's time to stretch out and get comfortable, dogs aren't shy about picking choice locations. A soft carpet in the middle of the room will work nicely. So will a comfortable leather couch or, on really cold nights, the warm comfort of a queen-size bed. And once they get settled, they're extremely reluctant to move. That's why owners often spend their days stepping gingerly over or around their recumbent canines, and their nights huddled on the edge of the bed while their indolent dogs spread out in dreamy comfort.

There's nothing wrong with letting sleeping dogs lie, but allowing them to dominate the family's space is one of the most common forms of miscommunication, says Yody Blass, director of Companion Animal Behavior in Ashburn, Virginia. You may feel it's simple courtesy to let your dog lounge in peace or to step back when she pushes her way past you in the hall. But to your dog, these are signals that she, more than you, is worthy of respect.

Dogs are extremely class-conscious. In the distant past, when dogs lived only with other dogs, their society was strictly hierarchical. Some dogs were leaders, others were followers. Each dog knew her place. The top dogs got the best places to sleep. They ate and drank first. And they expected other dogs to defer to them.

Most dogs don't live in canine packs any more, but they're still concerned about status. They're happy to obey those whom they perceive as holding a higher status. However, they're less likely to be quite so accommodating when they feel that the balance of power is shifting their way.

That means that when you step around your dog instead of telling her to move, or when you allow her to sleep in the bed or push past you on her way out the door, she'll begin thinking of

It's not only large dogs that occasionally try to rule the roost. Small dogs like this pug can also try to dominate the humans in their family, especially when they're allowed to take over the furniture.

herself as the top dog, Blass says. That could mean that she'll view you as her second banana. What began as a courtesy, in your mind, will be interpreted by your dog as a hint to take charge.

This can occur even in families where dogs don't sleep on the furniture. A dog who sleeps in a doorway and doesn't move when you approach is quietly testing the boundaries. You probably don't think twice of stepping around her, but over time she'll take this to mean that you're deferring to her and that her star is rising in the family hierarchy.

It's important to recognize this difference in perspective because dogs that start dominating space may try to dominate in other ways, as well. It all comes down to respect: You wouldn't stand in the President's way if he were approaching, and your dog shouldn't stand in your way, either, Myers says.

Vocal Signals

Dogs often misinterpret the way people speak to them. They don't find it easy to understand words alone, so they listen for other things, like the pitch and tone of your voice, to help them understand your meaning. This means you need to match these things to the content of your message to ensure that your dog knows what you mean. For example, people with high voices may need to make a special effort to sound forceful enough when they're giving a dog a command, says Greg Strong, a trainer in Easton, Maryland. If they don't, a dog may think that she doesn't really have to do what she's told—and respond accordingly. And people with deep voices may have difficulty pitching their voices high enough to convey pleasure and approval when they're praising a dog.

Words are most effective when they're said in the right tone of voice. This boxer knows that his owner's serious tone means a reprimand.

Dogs can also be confused when people use the wrong tone. For example, if you put a kind of question mark on the end of a command, your dog may not realize that you expect her to do something. Similarly, if you speak to her in too stern a tone, she may think you're unhappy with her, and so be reluctant to respond to you.

Another common source of confusion is a lack of expression in a person's voice. For example, if you praise your dog in the same brisk, no-nonsense tone that you use to give commands, she probably won't know that she's done something right, says Kovary. Instead, praise her in a high, happy, enthusiastic voice that will tell her clearly that she has pleased you.

Sending Clear Messages

Once you understand how dogs think, it's usually not difficult to speak and act in ways they can understand. It's worth making the effort because no matter how hard your dog tries to get along, human society is a lot different—and a lot more confusing—to her than it is to you. By communicating clearly and telling her exactly what's expected, she'll feel confident and will be more comfortable looking to you for direction.

Be consistent. If you were trying to learn Spanish, you'd be thoroughly befuddled if one day you were told adios means "hello" and the next day you were told it means "goodbye." Dogs run into this lack of consistency all the time. One day we shoo them from the table when they're begging for a hand-out, and the next day we say "just this once." Giving mixed signals creates a lot of confusion—along with a lot of mooching dogs.

Because she is praised the moment she drops the ball, this shiba inu understands that she's done the right thing.

The best way to avoid communication breakdowns is to be totally consistent, says Kovary. If you don't want your dog begging from the table, don't slip her food. Ever. If you don't want her on the couch, say "off," and be prepared to enforce it. Use exactly the same commands all the time. In learning to live with humans, dogs are essentially learning a new language, and giving consistent messages will make it easier for them to know what's expected.

Praise often. Dogs don't understand much human language and they can't read a list of rules. It's difficult for them to know what they are and aren't supposed to do. That's why it's crucial to give dogs a lot of praise when they do things right, says Kovary. When your dog steps out of your way when you walk to the door, tell her she's a good girl. Rub her head when she comes to your call, and give her a treat if she stops barking when you tell her to. No matter what form praise takes—a kind word, a stroke, or a biscuit—it makes it very clear to your dog

that she read your message loud and clear. It also tells her that you appreciate her efforts—and every dog loves to hear that.

Praise immediately. It's not always easy for dogs to make a mental connection between what you're telling them and what it relates to. "You've got about a three-second window in which your dog connects what you're doing or saying with what she's done," Blass explains. For praise to be effective, it has to be immediate.

Show her what you want. Few things are more frustrating than being told to do something, but not understanding what, exactly, you're supposed to do. Dogs go through this all the time. Like tourists who don't speak the language, they can tell from your tone of voice that you want something, but they haven't the slightest idea what it might be.

One of the quickest ways to get around communication barriers is to show your dog what you want, says Kovary. In other words, if you see your dog about to do something wrong, show her how to do something right.

For example, lead your dog outside when it looks as though she's going to make a pit stop on the carpet, and then praise her for going in the right place. If she doesn't move when you tell her to, nudge her out of the way. When she sniffs you where she shouldn't, step forward to make her back off, or give her the command "off." Combining commands with this type of direct reinforcement—along with praise when they do what you want—makes it much easier for dogs to understand what you're telling them.

CHAPTER NINETEEN

TEN COMMON COMMUNICATION PROBLEMS

Most of our dogs' behavior problems are simply a result of miscommunication. Once you work out what dogs are saying and find better ways to communicate with them, most behavior problems are easy to fix.

Dogs and people have been living together for thousands of years, and for the most part we understand each other pretty well. But every now and then we encounter situations in which communication breaks down. Our dogs don't understand what we want them to do, or, just as often, we give them messages we didn't intend.

When you consider that people and dogs speak entirely different languages, it's surprising that failures to communicate don't occur more often. "It's hard enough to communicate clearly and effectively with people," says Liz Thomas, a dog trainer in Alexandria, Virginia. "But when we try to communicate with our dogs, we have the added difficulty of working with a different species that doesn't talk and doesn't think the same way people do."

Communication problems sometimes take surprising forms, and it's not always easy to recognize them for what they are, Thomas says. Suppose your dog has been chewing on your shoes. She isn't merely misbehaving. She's trying to tell you something. What that something is depends on the dog and the situation. Dogs who spend a lot of time alone will sometimes chew

as a way of dispelling feelings of loneliness or frustration. Other dogs chew because they don't understand the difference between their possessions and yours. Others may chew for the simple reason that it feels good to do it.

In other words, people and dogs speak different languages—and until we each learn the other's language at least a little bit, we're bound

Consistent rules are necessary to avoid confusion. If you don't want your dog on some of the furniture, don't let her on any of it, including the beds.

to have communication problems. Often, these problems take surprising forms. You might not think that destructive chewing, leash-pulling, or housesoiling result from our failures to communicate with our dogs, or vice versa. In fact, communication may be at the heart of some of these difficulties.

In many cases, solving these problems gets a lot easier with a little bit of empathy on our part. Here are some ideas on how to better understand why your dog is doing something, and how to overcome some of the most frequently occurring—not to mention vexing—obstacles to human–canine harmony.

Aggression

Some dogs know what they want and will be very aggressive about getting it. They'll bump against their owners to demand attention. They'll take over certain spots in the house and nothing will induce them to move. They will

CALL FOR HELP

Even though aggression isn't necessarily any harder to change than other behavior problems, there isn't as much room for error. A dog who doesn't learn her lessons quickly may bite or threaten people, and that can be dangerous. That's why experts recommend calling a trainer or behaviorist at the first sign of aggressive displays, says Myrna Milani, D.V.M., a veterinarian and behaviorist in Claremont, New Hampshire.

insist on playing or being petted and won't take no for an answer. Essentially, they want to call all the shots.

Aggression can take more serious forms as well. It's not uncommon for dogs to growl or grumble—or in some cases, to bite—in order to have their own way. This type of aggression never goes away on its own. In fact, it's the most common behavior problem that sends owners to behaviorists and trainers looking for help.

Aggression is a complex problem because it can be caused by many different things. Some dogs simply have dominant personalities. Even if they never show signs of actual aggression, they'll always try to get their way. Other dogs may be insecure or angry. They're the ones most likely to growl or bite.

You can tell a lot about your dog's personality by the way she expresses her aggressive or dominant tendencies. Here's what the signals usually mean.

Hey, talk to me. It's fairly common for dogs to nudge or gently butt their owners simply because they want some attention. This type of behavior usually isn't a problem as long as dogs aren't acting pushy under other circumstances, says Pat Miller, a trainer in Salinas, California.

I want to be in control. Dogs that are always nudging people and who also play roughly, take over choice spots on the furniture, or refuse to move when their owners try to squeeze past are showing more serious forms of aggression. They want to be in charge, and they're taking steps to fortify their advantage. Unless you stop them quickly, they'll continue trying to be dominant and will get pushier and more difficult to be around.

This Labrador mix loves a game of Frisbee, in which she cooperates rather than competes with her owner. This type of play will help prevent her from trying to become the dominant member of the family.

Since biting, growling, and other forms of aggression can be quite dangerous—not only to you, but to other people as well—you may want to call a trainer for help. But the basic principles of "demoting" a dog and making her more cooperative aren't very difficult to apply.

For example, play games in which you and your dog cooperate, like throwing a ball or going for walks. Games such as tug-of-war, however, create a mood of competition, which only reinforces a dog's desire to come out on top.

Territory and possession can mean a lot to dogs, which is why aggressive behavior often includes taking over the furniture and refusing to move. As long as your dog is showing signs of aggression, you should keep her off the furniture all the time. Dogs see the furniture as a "choice" location, and by keeping them off, they'll come to understand that their position in the family is subordinate to yours.

Doorways are another form of territory, and you should make sure that your dog always goes through after you and not before. In addition, don't let her lounge in front of a doorway or a flight of stairs, says Robin Kovary, director of the American Dog Trainers Network in New York

POOCH ?? PUZZLER

Why do dogs like to tug?

Pulling on one end of a rope toy while their owner pulls on the other is a favorite game for many dogs. Why do they like it so much?

"A tug-of-war triggers a dog's competitive instincts," says Steve Aiken, an animal behaviorist in Wichita, Kansas. "In the wild, the dominant animal gets first crack at every resource, including food," Aiken explains. However, animals are constantly competing with one another to see who that dominant animal should be. A lowly member of the pack that tries to grab a piece of food from the leader, for instance, will trigger a tug-of-war. The winner gets the food—and a position at the top of the pecking order.

"This is the reason why you hear dog trainers recommend that you don't play tug-of-war with your dog," says Aiken. "If you lose, it's a signal that perhaps you aren't the leader any more. This can cause behavior problems further down the track."

Still, lots of people and dogs do enjoy a good game of tug, and if it's done right, no harm will come of it. "Just make sure that you're the one who always wins," says Aiken. If your dog is likely, through strength and tenacity, to get the upper hand, you're much better off playing a game of fetch, where your dog is obliged to obey you but has fun at the same time.

115

City. Your dog should happily give way to you, not the other way around.

Taking your dog for long walks or doing regular obedience work are superb ways to control aggression. It strengthens the bond between you and reinforces your role as the leader. It also will tire her out, and a tired dog is less likely to be aggressive, says Kovary.

Let your dog know there's no such thing as a free lunch, that it's her job to earn your attention. Don't give her anything—food, petting, or anything else—unless she does something for you first. Make her sit before going outside, or practice other commands before putting her food on the floor.

Barking

No one objects to a little barking, but some dogs have an awful lot to say. They bark at everything—bicyclists, cats, or the sound of moving drapes. Or they'll bark by the hour, apparently for no other reason than to hear themselves speak.

Barking is one of the most common behavior problems. It's also among the most serious, not only because it drives owners crazy but because neighbors who run out of patience may wind up contacting local law enforcement authorities. Yelling doesn't help because dogs often think you're barking back, Kovary says.

Barking can be an intractable problem, not only because it's a natural behavior but because dogs have a lot of different reasons for doing it. Here's what they may be saying.

Someone's coming! Like their owners, dogs are territorial—but instead of building fences,

This Jack Russell terrier is barking because she wants her owner to check something out. When her call is answered, she'll stop barking on her own.

they bark. This can be helpful when you want to know if someone's on your property, but it can be a real nuisance when it's directed at everything from cats to the postal carrier.

If your dog's definition of intruders is too inclusive, you may want to resort to diversionary tactics, says Shirley Sullivan, president of PR Dog, a training and dog day care center in Falls Church, Virginia. For example, when you see the postal carrier coming, keep your dog busy and focused on you by having her repeatedly sit and lie down, a practice trainers refer to as "puppy pushups." The idea is to keep your dog busy until the distraction goes away.

Don't forget I'm here. Some dogs rev up their barking when their owners are on the telephone or engaged in another activity that shuts them out of the field of attention. Again, this is an easy problem to correct. Sullivan recommends snapping the leash on your dog when you're about to get busy. If she starts barking, tug on the leash to get her attention and quiet her down. Most dogs will get the hint fairly quickly. Eventually, just putting on the leash before you make a telephone call will guarantee you a little peace.

SPEAK NOW!

Barking is as natural to dogs as talking is to people. No matter how much you try to discourage barking, it's hard for dogs to figure out what the problem is. That's why trainers often take the opposite approach. Rather than teaching dogs not to bark, they teach them when to start. "Getting a dog to bark on command is the key to training a dog to stop barking," says Sandy Myers, a trainer and director of Narnia Pet Dog Training in Naperville, Illinois.

First, find out what you can do to start your dog barking. Speaking in an excited tone may do it. Or try jumping up and down, running in place and waving your arms up and down, or just acting excited. When your dog starts to bark, praise her by telling her "good bark" or "good speak" and give her a treat. Keep doing this until just giving the command will set her off.

Once she barks on command, it's time to teach her to stop on command, says Myers.

Use the command to get her barking. Then, when she pauses between barks, give her a treat and tell her "good quiet." Dogs can't bark and chew at the same time, and most dogs will eagerly swap one activity for the other. Keep practicing this until your dog consistently stops barking when you give the "quiet" command.

The idea isn't to stop the barking entirely, Myers says. "We want our dogs to let us know when something is out of the ordinary. And some dogs need to get barking out of their system. But they also need to respond to the 'quiet' command."

Myers recommends practicing once a day, both to start barking and to stop it. "Your dog will get to do the barking she naturally wants to do, and you'll be teaching her to control it at the same time."

Dogs such as this vizsla can be taught to bark on command. By controlling when your dog does and doesn't bark, you'll have a much better relationship with your dog and with your neighbors.

117

Listen to me. Dogs get bothered by all sorts of things, and they respond by calling their owners the only way they know—by barking. This type of barking is normal and you don't want to stop it, Kovary says. Take a moment to check out what's going on. Once your dog sees you're on the scene, she'll feel less responsible and will probably stop barking on her own.

Begging for Attention

Dogs can be real gluttons for attention. This often means they're a bit anxious and fearful and in frequent need of reassurance. Or they may simply be accustomed to getting a lot of attention, and the more they get, the more they want. It's gratifying when your dog pushes his head against your hand for the occasional rub or lies close to you when you're relaxing, but no one enjoys being hounded by a canine "shadow" who can't bear to be alone even for a minute.

It's not difficult to teach dogs to be less demanding, but first you need to understand what they're telling you with all their clinging.

I'm insecure. Even the most self-sufficient dog has certain fears—of thunderstorms, for example, or the sound of firecrackers—that will send her in search of attention. There's nothing wrong with giving a frightened dog a little reassurance, but you don't want to make too big a deal of it. If you do, she may get the idea that there really is something to be afraid of—or at least she'll get in the habit of turning to you whenever she gets nervous.

"Don't go overboard with affection because that tells your dog it's okay to be scared," says Kovary. "You're reinforcing her fear."

This Belgian shepherd puppy is jumping up on her owner to get attention. There's nothing wrong with the occasional request, but some dogs won't leave their owners alone. That's when you have to figure out what's causing them to be so demanding.

Rather than just giving comfort, she recommends a more proactive approach. Think about the things that scare your dog silly. It may be thunderstorms or fireworks, or even the sound of a newspaper rattling. Whatever it is, think about ways to expose her to small doses.

Dogs who are afraid of thunderstorms, for example, can learn to cope with them when their owners make tape recordings of storms and play them back at very low volumes, rewarding their dogs as long as they stay calm and relaxed. The idea is to gradually decrease the "fear factor" by playing the recording a little bit louder every day. If your dog starts getting nervous, reduce the volume. But as long as she stays relaxed, keep giving her praise and treats. If you do this slowly—and it may take months of daily "exposure"—she'll probably get a little better, and less demanding of your attention.

I want to be in charge. "If a dog tends to be pushy in all sorts of situations, demands for attention may indicate that she wants to be in control," says Miller. Your dog needs to be taught to earn any attention you give her. For example, if she's demanding to be petted, she should be told to sit or lie down before she gets those loving strokes. It's also better to keep the petting session brief. That way, she learns to relax and be less controlling.

I'm bored. Dogs who don't have a lot to do will sometimes beg for attention merely because they can't think of anything else to do. For example, if you're working on a computer project at home, and your dog begins to nudge you persistently after several hours, she may be saying that she's tired of just lying around while you're crunching spreadsheets.

You really can't expect dogs to entertain themselves all the time, Miller says. Dogs are social creatures and they want to spend time with you more than anything else. This doesn't mean you should give in to their every demand, but you will have to remember to schedule some time when they can have your undivided attention. As long as you take them for walks or play with them for 30 to 40 minutes a day, and don't let them con you into giving them attention in between, they'll learn to wait for "their" time, Miller says.

Begging for Food

There isn't a dog on the planet who doesn't lobby for extra goodies now and then. But dogs who persistently beg for food or steal it when no one is looking aren't merely being greedy—they have something to tell you.

I'm hungry. It's hard to believe that a dog who tucks into one or two good meals a day will devote so much energy to mooching. But every dog needs different amounts of food, and it's possible that your dog is merely hungry. You may want to try moving the usual dinner hour forward an hour or two. Or you can divide her usual amount of food into three or four servings and dish it out more often. Dogs will often feel more satisfied when they get several small meals instead of one big one.

Pay attention to me. Dogs, like people, sometimes develop a strange relationship with food. In their mind it's the symbol of love and companionship, and they'll beg for food when what they really want is attention. "Never give your dog food from the table," Thomas says. "You don't want her to learn that pestering you

Begging for food is often your dog's way of saying "I'm hungry for attention." Give her some petting instead of a treat, and she will probably stop begging.

while you're eating will result in her getting a morsel or two. Rewarding such behavior can be the start of an annoying habit."

There's a simple technique that will discourage dogs from staking out the dining table. Choose a single spot where you want your dog to stay when you're eating. It could be in a corner of the dining room or in another room. Just be sure that you can see her while you're eating. Put her on a long lead, lead her to the "place," and give her a treat. If you do this every day, she'll learn that the easiest way to get food is to go to this spot on her own, Thomas says.

"Once your dog consistently goes to her place on command, teach her to lie down and stay in that place," Thomas says. The "down" command can be tricky at first, but here's an easy way to teach it: Hold a treat level with her eyes, then draw it downward and along the ground away from her. She will follow the treat with her eyes and automatically lie down. Give her the treat, tell her to stay, then sit down and enjoy your dinner.

At first you'll want to get up a few times to reward her for staying put. Once she understands that food comes to her, she'll be perfectly content to stay in her place and will be less likely to hit you up for food while you're eating.

I'm bored with my diet. Most dogs happily feast on the same food every day, but some get tired of having the same old thing, especially when there are more interesting food aromas to check out.

There's nothing wrong with periodically giving dogs new foods, but to avoid dietary upsets, do it gradually by adding the new

food or flavor to the current one in progressively greater proportions over a period of about one week. Try mixing some wet food in with the dry. Or add water to your dog's dry food to make a gravy. Even warming food slightly can stimulate a dog's tastebuds. Warm food releases more smells, and it's the smell of food more than the taste than gets dogs excited.

Climbing on the Furniture

Dogs enjoy getting comfortable, and a soft chair or comforter-topped bed is a much nicer place to catch 40 winks than the hard floor. But

Dogs love getting on furniture and they don't mind sharing it with the humans in the family. This Labrador mix finds the high vantage point makes it easy to see what's going on.

comfort isn't the only reason dogs take over the furniture. From their point of view, the human comfort zones are positions of power—more attractive by far than a bean bag on the floor. Which is why even dogs given the best accommodations will often sneak up on the couch or slip into your bed late at night. What are they trying to tell you?

I want to see what's going on. Nowhere is the realtor's mantra—"location, location, location"—more true than among dogs. They like to know what's happening around them and to be a part of things, even when they're only silent spectators. Unlike their own beds, which are usually tucked out of the way, couches and easy chairs are located in prime positions and offer great vantage points from which to see what's going on. In addition, furniture is relatively high off the ground, and high positions, among dogs, are considered prime status spots.

Once a dog appropriates a piece of furniture, it can be very difficult to persuade her to sleep elsewhere. Apart from using repellents, which often don't work very well, trainers recommend covering dogs' chosen spots with books or other impediments for a few days, while at the same time providing a more comfortable dog bed that's located in prime real estate—right next to the couch, for example, or near the center of the room, where she can see what's going on.

I thought it was okay! People don't always admit it, but trainers have found that furniture-

Canine Bed Testers

Dogs rely on their human friends to manufacture comfy sleeping places for them. But humans are at a distinct disadvantage: How can we tell which beds dogs like and which they don't?

Drs. Foster and Smith, a pet product manufacturing and catalog company based in Rhinelander, Wisconsin, has come up with a remarkably simple solution. They ask the dogs.

"Our employees take dog beds and fabric throws home with them and test them out on their own dogs," reports company spokesperson Candy Besaw. "That way they can see if the dog likes the item—especially the fabric that the bed is made from."

Candy's own dog, a wire-haired fox terrier named Linus, proved to be a legend because of his longevity at the company, bed-testing for most of his 21 years.

Linus and other senior dogs prefer thick foam beds that are easy to get into and out of. "Many older dogs have arthritis, and the foam beds are easy on their aches and pains," says Candy.

Other dogs have different choices. "Very small dogs seem to like oval-shaped cuddler-type beds, which are small and have high, soft sides," explains Candy. "But larger dogs prefer big cushions because they can stretch out on them."

hogging dogs are usually getting some surreptitious encouragement from someone in the family. No matter how often you tell your dog to get off the couch, she's going to keep getting up when someone else is encouraging her on the sly.

Dogs learn best when they get consistent messages from all the people in their lives. As long as everyone in the family takes a united stand—by warning them before they make their ascent onto the furniture, and immediately kicking them off on the occasions they get lucky—dogs will generally decide that it's not worth the bother and will cheerfully accept their own comfortable beds.

Destructive Behavior

Puppies will happily spend hours chewing shoes, wrecking table legs, or shredding jackets. Part of this is due to teething—chewing makes them feel better. And partly it's because chewing is fun, and they haven't yet learned to tell the difference between a rawhide bone and your new loafers. Most puppies go through teething between four and eight months of age.

What's normal behavior in puppies, however, is a sign of problems in older dogs. Here's what it probably means.

What else is there to do? Dogs will sometimes trash their owners' belongings simply because there's nothing better to do, says Kovary. It is especially common in dogs who spend a lot of time alone.

A Buster Cube keeps this vizsla occupied for hours. When he has a lot to do, he's less likely to look for other forms of entertainment— like destroying the house.

They get bored and start looking for excitement. And chewing is a fun diversion.

I'm scared to be alone. Dogs are social animals who don't like being alone. Most dogs learn to cope with it, but some get nearly frantic, and chewing and other forms of destructive behavior are their way of reducing feelings of loneliness and fear. "Your clothes and belongings have your scent on them," Kovary says. "Your dog will feel closer to you and less lonely if she chews on them and inhales some of that scent."

Regardless of what's causing your dog to chew, it's usually not that hard to make her stop, Thomas says. Probably the best solution is to buy a few chew toys—assuming, of course, that the toys are more appealing than your possessions. "The Kong toy is one of the best toys you can buy," Thomas says. "It's made of hard rubber and is virtually indestructible. And it's hollow inside so that it can be stuffed with treats to make it even more attractive."

Another great toy is the Buster Cube. These are hollow toys with hidden compartments you can fill with food. As dogs mouth the toy and push it around, bits of food will occasionally fall out.

The promise of food can keep dogs happily engaged for hours—and when they're playing with their own toys, they're less likely to show an interest in yours.

Dogs need more than toys to burn off excess energy. Regular exercise is essential, Thomas says. Dogs who wear themselves out on walks or by running around are much less likely to get bored and lonely. "A tired dog is a well-behaved dog," Kovary says.

Greeting Disorders

Nearly every dog gets excited when people come to visit, but some go completely overboard. They run around in circles, bark their heads off, or jump as high as they can, leaving dusty little paw prints on skirts and jackets. Even people who love dogs don't enjoy being greeted with so much exuberance, and they don't appreciate the intrusion of inquisitive noses into embarrassing places.

Apart from walks and meal times, most dogs don't have a lot of high points in their days, so it's not surprising that they get worked up when visitors drop by and liven things up. It's easy to train puppies to greet people with decorum, but it's more difficult to teach older dogs to behave more soberly. Not only are they set in their ways but also there may be other reasons for their assertive hellos. Here's what they're probably thinking.

I'm just being myself. Among people, the most socially unacceptable kind of dog greeting is to have a cold nose pushed into a private place. But among dogs, this is simply the way they do things, and they can't figure out why people get so uncomfortable. This is one situation where dogs and people will never see eye to

This golden retriever has been taught to sit when her owner opens the door to visitors. She's rewarded for this good behavior by being allowed to sniff the visitor's hand when she enters the house.

LICKETY SPIT

While a peck on the cheek is a common and acceptable form of greeting between humans, a sloppy, wet lick from a dog can send guests and owners ducking for cover.

"Licking often signals submissive or solicitous behavior," explains Steve Aiken, an animal behaviorist in Wichita, Kansas. "When they lick us, they may be acknowledging that we're their leaders."

When adult dogs greet each other, the more submissive one may greet the other by nudging his muzzle and sometimes licking around his lips, explains Linda Goodloe, a certified animal behaviorist in New York City. "Lip-smacking and lip-licking are considered pacifying behaviors," says Goodloe.

Licking can sometimes be a way of begging for food, too. When wolf puppies greet their mother after she's been hunting, they lick her muzzle to encourage her to regurgitate the food for them. Fortunately, in domesticated dogs licking is more a sign of respect than a request for a meal.

eye without some training, Kovary says. You should never let your dog put her nose in people's crotches, she advises. When your dog makes her move, quickly tell her "off" or "no," and do it every time. "Once your dog has calmed down and is sitting quietly, you can let her satisfy her curiosity by sniffing your guests' hands," she says.

I'm ambivalent about this. Dogs tend to get most excited when they're of two minds about guests arriving, says Kovary. On the one hand, they're happy and eager to greet the person entering the house.

This Brittany spaniel always gets over-excited when visitors come. To keep her under control, her owner puts her on a short leash beforehand and gives her a treat when she behaves.

INTRODUCING YOURSELF

Most of us have learned to greet dogs by putting out our hand with the palm down, giving them a chance to sniff the back. There's nothing wrong with this approach, but some experts believe that it's better to greet dogs with your palm up.

"The palm of your hand emits a positive electric charge, whereas the back of your hand emits a negative electric charge," says Wendy Volhard, a professional trainer in Phoenix, New York. A positive charge attracts dogs and a negative one repels them, she explains.

But they're also wondering how this new person will fit into the group, and they aren't quite sure how to respond. So they display a whole variety of behaviors—jumping up, barking, and so on—as a way of "testing" how this new person is going to react to them.

An easy solution is to distract your dog as soon as people arrive. One way to do this is to make her lie down straight away. By going into training mode, you will focus attention more on you than on the new arrivals. When she does what you tell her, give her a treat, Kovary adds. It won't take her long to learn that acting calmly and following commands gets her something good to eat. Of course, this will make your dog look forward to visitors even more, but she will also know that gracious greetings bring better rewards than rambunctious jumping.

Some dogs get the message right away, but others need more work. Thomas recommends putting dogs on a six-foot leash before people come over. As guests arrive, you can either stand on the leash or take up most of the slack in your hands. "She won't have enough leash to allow her

CALL FOR HELP

No one enjoys finding spots on the carpet or puddles in the kitchen, but occasional "accidents" are a normal part of owning a dog. What isn't normal is when a dog who's always had control is suddenly making messes all the time.

Frequent housesoiling is often the first sign of physical problems, says Christine Wilford, D.V.M., a veterinarian in private practice in Seattle. Dogs with urinary tract infections, for example, may have to urinate several times an hour, and if you aren't there to let them out, they'll do what they have to do. Other conditions that can cause a loss of control include diabetes, bladder stones, or an intestinal problem. A few accidents are unlikely to be signs of serious problems, but you should call your vet if your dog isn't back to normal within a few days.

in. "Try placing a bag of treats outside your front door and put a sign on it that says, 'These treats are for our dog—but only if she is sitting when you come in,'" Thomas suggests. Most people will get a kick out of joining in, and your dog will learn more quickly as more and more people participate.

Housesoiling

Dogs are usually house-trained by the time they are a few months old, and once they know the rules, they'll do everything they can to reach their favorite spots in time. But even dogs with perfect track records will occasionally go where they shouldn't. These aren't really "accidents" because grown dogs know that they're supposed to go outside. Dogs who go in the house are invariably trying to tell you something.

I couldn't wait. Even dogs with fastidious manners and good training have certain limits. Unless you have a doggy door, they can't let themselves out when nature calls. When you're

feet to rise more than three inches off the floor," Thomas says. "There's no risk of her jumping around or sniffing your guests."

Greeting problems can be awkward because you can't deal with them in private—you have to get used to training your dog at a time you'd rather be concentrating on your guests. But the slight social awkwardness will pay off fairly quickly, especially if you ask your guests to join

Adult dogs rarely make messes in the house unless there's something wrong. But for puppies, waiting to go outside may be more than they can handle.

gone all day or working late, it's simply not realistic to expect them to wait, says Mike Richards, D.V.M., a veterinarian in private practice in Cobbs Creek, Virginia.

For most dogs, Richards says, 12 hours is about the limit. When you're going to be gone longer than that, the only solution is to make other arrangements—having a neighbor let your dog out, for example, or hiring a pet sitter to drop by once a day.

I'm in charge, and here's the proof. Among dogs, urinating represents more than a comfort stop. It's also their way of marking territory and establishing their status in the family. That's why people who get a second pet are often subjected to an outbreak of housesoiling as one of the dogs—usually the older resident—begins urinating in strategic spots.

It may take a few weeks or longer for both dogs to feel comfortable with the new arrangement, says Sandy Myers, a trainer and director of Narnia Pet Training in Naperville, Illinois. You can speed things up by reinforcing the natural pecking order. Give special preference to the "top dog"—which is usually, but not always, the one who's been there the longest. Try feeding this dog first, she advises. Let her go out the door first, and give her the most attention. Once your dog feels that her status in the family is secure, she'll be much less inclined to defend it on her own, Myers explains.

I worship the ground you walk on. When a dog rolls on her back the minute you come home and then urinates on the floor, she's not forgetting her housetraining and she's not being rude. In fact,

she's doing the opposite. "Such a dog is being superpolite," explains Kovary. "She's saying, 'I know that you are my leader and I will do anything you ask.'" Called submissive urination, this is very common among dogs, Kovary explains. But it's not a good sign in the family because it means a dog is overly anxious or intimidated. About all you can do is try to make sure that your dog is more secure. There are a lot of ways to do this. For example, don't stand over her and look down when you first get home—kneel down and greet her from a more "equal" level, Thomas suggests. It's also a good idea to avoid direct eye contact for a while because some dogs find it intimidating.

Extreme submissive behavior isn't easy to fix because it can be an intrinsic part of a dog's personality. If simple changes don't help, you may want to call your vet or a trainer for help.

This Labrador retriever gets plenty of praise from her owner when she responds quickly to his commands. This reinforces her obedient behavior.

Dogs easily get distracted by all the exciting things around them, and this makes it hard for them to pay attention.

Ignoring Commands

We all tune each other out sometimes, and dogs are no different. But sometimes they deliberately ignore their owners' requests. Here are some of the reasons why.

I don't understand. Giving a command the wrong way is a recipe for confusion. "Unless you're clear, brief, and consistent, your dog may not understand what you want of her," says Greg Strong, a trainer in Easton, Maryland.

"Some people tell a dog to sit, but then they put a kind of question mark at the end—like they're asking her to sit instead of telling her to. If you do that, your dog may not obey the command," says Strong.

Use brief, one- or two-word commands, he advises. "Be careful to use the same word or words every time, and be sure to use a distinctive, upbeat tone of voice."

What's in it for me? Dogs know they're supposed to obey, but sometimes there's no way they'll drop a bone or run back to their owners unless something good is going to come out of it. As far as they're concerned, the merits of ignoring their owners may outweigh the benefits of complying.

Owners who don't praise their dogs enough will soon find that their dogs "forget" to obey, says Kovary. Just like people, dogs need an incentive to continue doing their jobs. For most dogs, these jobs are to do what their owners tell them, and the reward should be enthusiastic, immediate praise—whether that praise comes in the form of a treat, a pat, or an exuberant "Good dog!" explains Kovary.

I'm afraid of what you'll do if I do what you tell me. If every command were followed by something exciting and fun, there would be a lot more attentive dogs. But in the real world, commands such as "come" or "down" can often indicate that something unpleasant, like a bath, is about to occur. Dogs have long memories, and the ability to put two and two together. Once a dog makes the connection between "come" and "bath," she will be likely to ignore you in the future.

It's a good idea to follow any command with an action that pleases your dog, Kovary says. This is important if you want her to come when you call her. In fact, it's a good idea to never call a dog to you when you know you're going to do something she'll dislike, like giving her a bath or crating her. In these cases, it's better to go to her rather than expect her to come to you.

Hey, things look interesting over there.
Some dogs tune out their owners occasionally because there's too much else going on. Distractions, and maybe a bit of daydreaming, can result in some commands going unheeded.

I can't hear you. Dogs who have suddenly quit responding to commands or only respond to them occasionally may be going a little bit deaf. To see if your dog is hard of hearing, stand a few feet behind her and clap your hands. If she doesn't react, you'll need to get her to a vet.

I don't have to listen to you. Dogs are very status-conscious. They want to know who is the leader and who isn't. If they don't know, they'll assume that they are and will pay less and less attention to their owners.

You cannot have an effective relationship with your dog unless you are willing to take on the role of leader. That involves giving commands and following through on them. Make sure that you're consistent in the messages you give your dog. Don't let her be bratty or aggressive. And when she wants something, make sure she earns it first by doing something you've told her to do.

Dogs are a lot like children in that it doesn't take them long to discover your weaknesses. Many people, for example, tell their dogs "come," but they don't really expect them to come right away, and their dogs certainly don't feel like rushing over. So they tell them "come" again, and a third time, and their dogs still don't come—because their owners have inadvertently taught them that it's okay to ignore them. The only way to prevent this is to only give commands that you're able and willing to enforce, Thomas says.

Pulling on the Leash

We've all seen people flash past whose dogs were clearly taking them for a walk rather than the other way around. Dogs that pull constantly on the leash can turn an enjoyable stroll into a shoulder-wrenching marathon. As with other forms of misbehavior, bad leash manners are your dog's way of saying something. It's important to discover why your dog is pulling on the leash, so that you can find the right solution.

This schnauzer clearly feels that it's his duty to take his owner for a walk. One of the easiest ways to reverse the situation is to suddenly turn around and walk the other way. This will force the dog to follow rather than lead.

This German shepherd mix is given time to check things out when she goes on walks with her owner. Because she has time to investigate, she's less likely to pull ahead.

I'm in charge here. Dogs who pull on the leash have somehow gotten they idea that they, not you, are in control. This usually occurs in families where the people haven't firmly established that they—not their dog—are the ones calling the shots.

Gotta check this out. From a dog's point of view, anything new is intriguing, and anything intriguing is worth investigating. Sights and sounds that mean nothing to people serve as magnets to dogs.

Gotta get that squirrel. Some dogs strain at the leash whenever they see a smaller animal nearby. Dogs used to be predators, and their instincts tell them to respond to movements by going forward themselves.

Let's get where we're going as fast as we can. Enthusiasm isn't just a human emotion. When dogs know they're on the way to some-thing exciting, they may pull on the leash in an attempt to get there sooner.

I'm so excited. Sometimes when a dog isn't taken out for a walk on a regular basis, she'll be so excited every time she does go for a walk that she'll always pull ahead. The best way to avoid this is to take your dog for a walk every day, even if you don't need to walk her for bathroom breaks.

When this isn't practical, arrange for a friend, neighbor, or professional dog walker to take your dog for a walk. This way your dog won't be so excited and will be less inclined to pull ahead.

Regardless of why dogs pull on the leash, the underlying message is the same: They feel that whatever is happening around them or what they're feeling at the moment is more important than worrying about you.

To curtail their penchant for pulling, you have to distract them from whatever it is that's grabbing their attention and get them to focus on you and you alone, says Shirley Sullivan, president of PR Dog, a training and dog day care center in Falls Church, Virginia.

There's an easy way to do this, says Sullivan. "If your dog lunges ahead of you while you're walking, immediately turn around and walk in the opposite direction. This will surprise your dog—and dogs generally don't like such surprises."

After a few weeks of subjecting your dog to these unexpected turns of events, she will begin watching you so she won't be surprised the next time. And the more she watches and keeps pace with you, the more pleasant your walks are going to be.

PART FIVE

PUTTING IT TO WORK

Knowing how dogs communicate—with other dogs as
well as people—provides a tremendous edge in understanding
what they're trying to say. You can use their language, which includes
not only sounds, but also touch and smells, to form a deeper
bond and help them behave a little better.

CHAPTER TWENTY

TEACHING YOUR DOG

Dogs love to learn new things, so teaching your dog
not only makes him easier to live with, it also keeps
him busy and makes him feel useful.

Dogs can do some truly amazing things. They find people who are lost, guide those who are blind, and act as the ears of people who are deaf. They can detect drugs and explosives. They've even been used to help prevent plane crashes.

Unfortunately, some dogs have abilities that aren't so useful. Like the bearded collie who thinks it's great fun to bark at delivery trucks. Or the German shepherd who builds towers in the backyard, using cans of cat food he's filched from the kitchen cupboard. Or the springer spaniel who's learned to open the refrigerator and eat all the food inside.

Both groups of dogs are intelligent and talented, capable of carrying out complex tasks. The difference is that the first group of dogs has been taught by people to do things that people find useful. Those in the second group, however, lacking human guidance, have taught themselves to do things *they* think are useful. Their owners, of course, may have a somewhat different opinion about what is and isn't helpful.

Dogs need to be busy, and this golden retriever mix gets a lot of satisfaction from fetching the newspaper every morning.

Why Dogs Need to be Taught

When you see your dog snoozing away the better part of the day, it's hard to believe that dogs like to be busy. But inside every dog is an instinctive need to do a good day's work. "Dogs were never bred to just be our pals," says Deborah Loven Gray, of Washington, D.C.,

author of *Your Dog's Life.* On the contrary, dogs have been bred for thousands of years to perform specific tasks, such as hunting, guarding, herding, or retrieving. "And if he's a mixed breed, a dog can combine more than one of these purposes," says Robin Kovary, director of the American Dog Trainers Network in New York City.

Whatever their breed, dogs have a genetic need to be busy all day, every day. When they're not busy doing something—anything—they easily become bored. When that happens they look for whatever kind of entertainment they can find, and their idea of fun—chewing on furniture, digging up the yard, or barking out the window all day—is unlikely to be the same as yours.

Even though most dogs will never be trained for police work or to do search and rescue, basic training gives them a purpose. Doing something as simple as teaching your dog to sit or walk on a leash will give him a sense of direction. Rather than being bored and frustrated, he'll be excited and fulfilled because he has a job to do, and he'll do his best to please you.

Dogs also need training because they see the world in ways humans can hardly understand. What comes naturally to them is totally out of

place among the humans in their lives. Among dogs, for example, it's accepted, even expected, for one dog to defend his food by snarling at or biting an interloper, says Pat Miller, a trainer in

PUPPY DOG TALES

The $58,000 Dog

Of all the extraordinary things that dogs can do, perhaps none is as amazing as preventing airplane crashes. Yet that's precisely what Jackie, a five-year-old Border collie, does every day.

Jackie lives and works at the Willow Grove Naval Air Station Joint Reserve Base near Philadelphia, Pennsylvania. Before she arrived, the base was struggling with a problem common to many airports: close encounters between aircraft and birds. At Willow Grove, the bothersome birds were Canada geese. Repeated collisions between planes and geese had caused $58,000 in damage to the expensive military aircraft over a five-year period. Despite some very creative attempts to solve the problem, including such things as setting off fireworks, shooting water cannons at the geese, and playing tapes of birds in distress, the Willow Grove geese proved difficult to evict—until Jackie was recruited.

Border collies were originally bred to herd sheep, but Jackie's mission is to herd geese away from the base's runways. Every time someone in the base control tower spots geese in the neighborhood, an air traffic controller radios the firehouse where Jackie lives. Then the real action begins.

Jackie is driven to where the geese are and set loose. "Jackie tries to corral the geese, the way she would with sheep," says Dave Bumm, one of Jackie's handlers. But the geese, unlike sheep, fly away. This is perfect for protecting the planes, but always leaves Jackie a bit unsatisfied. So to keep her happy, Bumm and the other handlers give her plenty of praise and play ball with her back at the firehouse.

Jackie's been on the job for over a year, and in that time there have been no collisions on her watch, compared with three bird strikes in the 18 months before she arrived.

Salinas, California. Among humans, however, the same behavior won't be tolerated. Training is the only way to help dogs understand what's expected of them and to give them clear guidelines for what they should and shouldn't do.

Giving Clear Signals

Most dogs enjoy learning new things, so there's no reason to settle for dry-as-dust backyard drill sessions once or twice a day. Dogs, like people, learn quickly and have the most fun when they bring all their senses into play.

By using a combination of words, sounds, hand signals, touch, and other forms of communication, you can teach your dog all the basics, and more, in a relatively short time. After that you can take advantage of his new-found skills to find other ways in which the two of you can communicate more clearly and so build a better relationship.

Words. Dogs may not be gifted linguists, but they can still learn a variety of words. Not surprisingly, the words they remember best are those that they associate with positive, pleasurable things. That's why trainers recommend rewarding dogs lavishly, with praise or tidbits to eat, when they first start responding to spoken commands. You don't have to give them treats every time, but when your dog's first starting out, linking words and treats will help him learn more quickly.

Sounds. Dogs respond to more than just words. They have much better hearing than humans do, and they also depend on their hearing more than we do. This means that sounds we tend to ignore—like the tone of someone's voice

A gentle touch on this vizsla's rump, combined with a verbal command, is his signal to stand still.

or a throat clearing—come through loud and clear for them. You can use these and other sounds, like clapping your hands, to reinforce spoken commands or merely to let your dog know he's done something right.

Hands. Dogs are a lot more responsive to body language than they are to words, which means that hand signals are a very effective way to convey messages. These silent, visual signals are helpful for adding emphasis or extra meaning when you're teaching your dog to understand certain words. In fact, you can train your dog to respond entirely to hand signals. This is particularly helpful for communicating across long distances, or if your dog becomes deaf as he gets older.

Touch. Dogs are extremely responsive to touch—whether they're doing the touching or being touched. You can use touch simply to keep your dog calm and relaxed, which will help him enjoy learning even more. Getting him used to some touches that he may not normally like will make him a lot easier for the vet or groomer to deal with. Touch will also help reinforce verbal commands, such as stand. Or you can use touch to teach your dog the sorts of touches that you do and don't like.

Touch works both ways, of course, and part of training is learning your dog's touch vocabulary. Every dog uses touch differently, but there are a few general rules. A muzzle that nuzzles into your hand, for example, can be a request for affection or an invitation to play. A dog that brushes against you may be asking for a loving touch—or he may be saying "Step aside, I have the right of way."

Scent. Dogs have a phenomenally sharp sense of smell, and smell is their primary means of communication, at least when they're with other dogs. That's why it makes sense for us to use scent as a way of communicating with them. Using scents that dogs don't like is a good way to tell them to leave certain things—like the furniture or the trash can—alone. Unpleasant scents can also tell them to stop barking. And we can use scents that dogs do like to help them deal with new situations, to introduce new people, and to provide comfort when we can't be with them.

A Nose for Diagnosis

Many retirees use the end of one career to pursue a second line of work. That's how George, a schnauzer who started out as a bomb-sniffing dog in Tallahassee, Florida, found himself using his sniffing skills to detect a different kind of danger.

George's second career began when a dermatologist in Tallahassee, Florida, Armand Cognetta, read a medical news report about a British woman whose dog persistently sniffed a mole on her skin, which later turned out to be cancer. Dr. Cognetta found himself wondering if dogs really could smell cancer, and if they could, whether they could be trained to detect it. So he teamed up with a trainer named Duane Pickel to see if Pickel's prize-winning dog, George, could be as successful at sniffing out skin cancer as he'd been at sniffing out bombs for the Tallahassee Police Department.

"Dogs need to have a purpose in life, and George loves to go to work and do new things," says Pickel. To train George, Pickel took him through a series of increasingly difficult tests, from retrieving melanoma samples stored in test tubes to detecting a cancer sample that had been placed under one of many band-aids on a volunteer's body. Finally, he put George to the true test by allowing him to sniff real cancer patients. On Pickel's command "show me," George would place a paw on the spot that he'd sniffed out. In most cases George was able to identify suspicious spots that doctors had believed to be cancerous, but hadn't yet been tested by biopsies.

COMMANDS EVERY DOG SHOULD KNOW

Dogs have an amazing capacity to learn commands. Highly trained show, working, and service dogs often know dozens of commands, including words, sounds, and signals. Most pet dogs are taught with vocal commands, but hand signals or nonvocal sounds are also effective. Whatever method you choose, most dogs only need to know 11 simple commands to get along happily with you and the rest of the world.

This German shepherd–Labrador cross has been trained to sit and stay, so his owner can trust him to wait patiently until she comes out of the shop.

Wait. Some dogs have a way of pushing their way to the front of the line when they want to go through doors or down narrow hallways. Telling them "wait" lets them know they're not supposed to go until you tell them to.

Sit. This is one of the easiest commands to teach, and also one of the most useful. Dogs who know how to sit are less likely to be jumping on you or anyone else, fighting with other dogs, or dragging you across the street at a red light.

A dog who knows how to heel correctly, like this shiba inu, will always walk nicely at his owner's side, rather than pulling her down the street.

Down. Like "sit," the "down" command is an essential part of doggy etiquette. It's also more comfortable than a sitting position when your dog is going to be hanging out for more than a minute or two.

Stay. Often paired with "sit" or "down," the "stay" command tells dogs to cool their jets for a while. It's not the easiest command for many dogs to learn because they'd rather be moving around than staying still.

Heel. Unless you live in the country and your dog never sees a busy road or walks on a leash, he has to understand this command. "Heel," or a variation such as "let's go," simply means that your dog will walk by your left side without lagging behind or lunging ahead. It's especially important for large dogs to understand "heel" because otherwise their relentless tugging on the leash will make going for walks seem too much like work.

Come. This is a crucial command in your dog's repertoire. Dogs who understand "come" will turn on a dime and head back to you as soon as you say it. It's a command you can use to keep them from running into the street or knocking into people in the park. It will tell them to come back when they'd just as soon keep running.

Stand. This command tells your dog to quit fidgeting and be still. It's useful for when you're grooming him, bathing him, checking him over, or drying him off on a wet day.

Off. Rare is the dog that doesn't prefer an expensive sofa or a goose-down comforter to his own bed. Dogs that understand "off" won't necessarily stay off the furniture, but at least they'll get off quickly when they know the command. "Off" also tells them not to jump up on you or other people.

Okay. Dogs love this command. "Okay" means they've done a good job. It means you're done giving orders and they can just act silly for a while. It may even mean it's time for dinner.

Out. Dogs know a good thing when they see it (and taste it), and getting them to relinquish such delicacies as a bone from the trash or your leather loafers can be a challenge when they haven't properly learned "out." This command means they should drop whatever it is that's in their mouth. They won't necessarily like it, but they'll do it as long as you start teaching them "out" when they're young.

Bed. This command, or a variation such as "crate," tells your dog that it's time to head for his sleeping place. It's useful not only at bedtime, but also when you want him to quiet down for a while.

This Australian kelpie mix knows that when his owner says "off," it's time to surrender his place on the sofa.

CHAPTER TWENTY-ONE

CHOOSING THE RIGHT NAME

What you call your dog is a very personal choice. You'll have to live
with the name for 10 or 15 years, so it pays to choose one you both like and
that your dog will find easy to learn and a pleasure to respond to.

When President Clinton welcomed his new chocolate Labrador into the White House in late 1997, thousands of Americans offered him ideas on what to name his dog. The president found himself sifting through proposals ranging from "Arkinpaws" to "Shoes" before he made his choice.

Like countless other dog owners, the president found that there's much more to naming a new dog than polling people for ideas. A range of factors, from personal associations to your dog's own response, should be considered when deciding on a name.

Ultimately, that's just what President Clinton did. The name he eventually chose for his new dog—Buddy—not only reflected his special memories of his late and much-loved Uncle Buddy, but it was also the name he felt his dog responded best to.

Most experts think the president was on the right track. In choosing a name for his dog, President Clinton made a lot of the right moves.

When to Use Human Names

Many people like to give human names to their dogs. President Clinton is just one case in point; a look at dog license registrations in any city,

Each of these chocolate Labrador puppies deserves a name that reflects his individuality and uniqueness.

town, or county provides countless others. Human names bestowed on dogs include Max, Maggie, Molly, Pepper, Brandy, Ginger, Sam, and Jake.

Trainers are divided on whether dogs should be given human names. The Monks of New Skete, who breed and train dogs at their monastery in Cambridge, New York, and are the authors of *How to Be Your Dog's Best Friend*, don't favor human names for dogs. The monks believe that giving dogs human names makes owners think of their dogs as people rather than animals, says Father Marc of New Skete.

But most trainers feel it doesn't really matter what you name your dog as long as the two of you are comfortable with it. "Your relationship with your dog is more important than his name," says Robin Kovary, director of the American Dog Trainers Network in New York City.

But whatever name you choose—human or not—the most important thing is to make sure it's appropriate to your dog's breed, gender, and size. By doing so, you recognize your dog's uniqueness and his distinctive personality, says Father Marc.

How to Make the Right Choice

Many people look for names that reflect their own expectations rather than their dog's personality, says Myrna Milani, D.V.M., a veterinarian and animal behaviorist in Claremont, New Hampshire, and author of *The Weekend Dog* and *Dog-Smart*. That can lead to poor name choices, such as a joke name or one that will cause people to react inappropriately to the dog, either with laughter or fear.

For example, Rambo is a poor choice for a pit bull terrier because it plays up the breed's aggressive image, and so may make another person fear the dog, no matter how friendly he

NAMES YOU SHOULD NEVER CHOOSE FOR YOUR DOG

Dogs are remarkably adaptable, so it's pretty hard to choose a name that will warp them for life. But there are some names, trainers say, that simply don't work—those that make fun of the dog, that could be confused with other words or commands, or that contain a sound dogs simply don't like. For example:

Moe. Sounds too much like "no!"

Helen. A dog may confuse it with "hello."

Sassy. Dogs dislike "s" sounds, probably because they resemble a snake's hiss.

Killer. For large dogs with tough reputations, a macho name will make them seem more frightening to other people. For small dogs like toy poodles or Chihuahuas, it will just sound silly.

Tiny. Every dog, whether he's big as a horse or small enough to fit in a teacup, thinks of himself as a big dog. Why hurt his feelings?

really is. And Tiny is a bad choice for a large breed such as a Great Dane because it makes fun of the dog's size.

It's also important to make your dog's name easy for him to learn. Father Marc suggests choosing a two-syllable name that begins with a strong consonant, such as Kirka or Jilly. Your

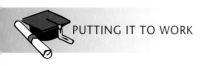

pup or dog will learn this type of name more quickly. That's because a long name, with three or more syllables, may be too complicated for a dog to learn easily, while a one-syllable name may sound too similar to parts of words that are used in everyday speech. This can cause confusion and make the name difficult for a dog to learn. A two-syllable name, however, will be easier for him to distinguish from all the other words he hears.

And avoid using names that sound too much like commands, advises Kovary. A good example is "Juno," which a dog could easily confuse with the word "no."

There are many names to choose from, from the commonplace to the exotic. Here are a few other things to consider before you decide.

Watch your dog for ideas. It's always good to look to your dog himself for ideas on a name, says Dr. Milani. If he's constantly sniffing out his environment, a name like Sherlock might be a good choice for your canine detective. For a dog who likes to run, Dasher could be the perfect moniker.

There's one exception to this principle, though. If your dog is a Rottweiler, Doberman, pit bull, or other breed with an aggressive reputation, you should avoid giving him an equally aggressive name. "The name could end up being a self-fulfilling prophecy," Kovary says. For example, a Rottweiler named Terminator who runs up to greet people may get a fearful reaction when they hear his name. When he senses their fear, his own response may be

more negative than it would be if he had a less aggressive-sounding name.

Choose a name that feels good to your dog. It's also important to consider a dog's preferences when deciding on his name. For example, most dogs dislike hearing an "s" sound, because it's like an unpleasant hiss, says Dr. Milani. She recommends trying out a few different names and sounds on your dog to find out which ones he responds best to.

Choose a name that feels good to you. It's important to give your dog a name that you like a lot. Dogs pay attention to your body language and the tone of your voice. If your dog can tell you feel good when you say his name, he'll be more likely to respond happily when he hears it.

Whether your dog is a dachshund or a Great Dane, his name should be appropriate to his breed and size. Giving him a name that pokes fun at his physical features might upset him by causing people to laugh at him.

Make it dignified. Naming a dog isn't a time to get funny or cute. "To use excessively sweet or joke names demeans both the dog and the relationship," says Father Marc. Dubbing your dachshund Frank or Weiner may seem funny at first, but the laughter that will follow whenever you call him could lead to problems. A dog who feels he's being laughed at may act aloof or uncertain around the person who's laughing. To him, the laughter appears mystifying or even hostile.

Overly cute or sentimental names can also cause problems. A German shepherd named Cuddles might pull his ears back or look away when he hears his name because he dislikes the laughter that it sometimes prompts.

Using Your Dog's Name for the Best Effect

After you've christened your pooch, you need to make sure you use his name effectively and appropriately. A frequent mistake people make is to use their dog's name not only to call him, but also in ordinary conversation with friends and family. When that happens too often, your dog may tune you out and stop responding when you call his name, says Dr. Milani. The solution is to find more than one way to refer to your pet, especially if he's within earshot. For example, if you're talking about your dog while he's lying at your feet, it's better to refer to him as "my guy" or "my pal" instead of by name.

It's also important to make sure you don't use your dog's name when correcting him.

This miniature schnauzer responds happily to his name because it's only used for pleasant things, like praise or to go for a walk, never for correcting him.

That's because your dog will respond more happily and promptly to his name if it always means that something wonderful is about to happen, like a walk or something to eat.

When you catch your dog doing something he shouldn't, it's best to use a simple, concise command such as "off!" or "leave it!" to correct him, rather than using his name in a stern tone as a kind of reprimand.

The most important thing is to use your dog's name in ways that make your high regard for him clear to him and to others. "A dog is sharply aware of changes in your voice tonality, facial expression, and body language," says Father Marc. "The more intelligent a dog is, the more sensitive he'll be to his owner's attitudes."

141

CHAPTER TWENTY-TWO

CHOOSING THE RIGHT COMMANDS

A well-behaved dog is a pleasure to have around. But before
you can train your dog to be a model canine citizen, you need to know
which commands are the right ones to use—and why.

Few people enjoy getting bossed around or being told to do something right away. We prefer a system where everyone is equal and every opinion carries the same weight.

If we lived in a world ruled by dogs, however, we'd have a very different perspective. Dogs aren't concerned with being autonomous. In fact, that's the last thing they want. What they care most about is being part of a family, whether that family consists of other dogs or the people in their lives. Taking orders, from a dog's point of view, is part and parcel of belonging; it makes them feel secure because it lets them know exactly where they stand.

This four-month-old Labrador–Scottish terrier cross is learning good manners while she's young—the best time for learning.

That's why you're doing your dog a favor when you teach her to obey commands. You may feel you're cramping her style at times, but she really wants you to tell her what to do. Giving orders—whether they're a simple "sit" or "down" command or a demand to get off the couch—makes it possible for her to know exactly what's expected, and she'll find a lot of reassurance in that.

Paradoxically, dogs that are comfortable obeying commands generally have more freedom than those without any training at all, says Pat Miller, a trainer in Salinas, California. A dog who comes reliably when you call will be able to enjoy more off-leash playtime than her less obedient friends. When she doesn't jump on people, she's more likely to be invited to join the crowd when you have visitors over. And when she's well behaved, she'll be allowed to spend more of her time with you, rather than being exiled to the backyard.

Every dog needs to know a few basic commands. But there's more to giving orders than saying "come" or "down." Some commands are a lot more effective than others. In order to choose the best commands, you have to think like a dog for a moment, because your dog's idea of a good command is going to be a little different from yours.

Clear Commands

Most dogs have good intentions. They want to please their owners and are unhappy when they don't. So why are there so many disobedient dogs? Most of the time it's because their owners haven't learned to communicate very well. The dogs want to obey; they just can't figure out what they're supposed to do. Here are a few ways to customize your commands in ways your dog will understand.

Get her attention. One reason dogs sometimes misbehave and ignore commands is that they don't realize they're being talked to. When you're playing in the park, your dog will be having such a good time running and sniffing that a shouted "come" may not enter her consciousness—which is why trainers advise coupling a command with a word that's guaranteed to get your dog's attention. A sure

A dog who can be trusted always to come when she's called, like this vizsla, will be able to have much more freedom than a dog who's not so reliable.

attention-getter is to use your dog's name, as in "Maggie! Come!"

Keep it short. Dogs aren't fluent in people-speak. They don't understand involved explanations or multi-sentence pleas because they can't pick out the one relevant word in a long stream of sound. That's why a command like "Maggie, will you please come here for once?" is likely to get you nothing more than a blank stare. What dogs do understand are short, quick commands, like "come" or "sit."

Make it firm. Our instincts are always to be polite, even when giving a command. But this doesn't work with dogs because what should sound like a command—"Maggie, sit!"—often sounds more like a question. In your dog's mind, you're asking, not telling, her to do something, and she won't see any reason to respond because in her mind she's not being told to.

Making commands short and terse is the best way to let your dog know that you want something, and you want it now. Dogs don't

143

This toy poodle understands he's done something wrong because his owner is using a firm tone of voice to correct him.

resent this tone of voice. On the contrary, they're always grateful when we make our expectations clear.

Be positive. Dogs are the Norman Vincent Peales of the animal kingdom—they thrive on positive thinking. More importantly, it's easier for them to understand positive commands—telling them what you want them to do—than negative ones, in which you simply say "no!" Suppose, for example, your dog is barking at the mailman. Yelling "no!" will get her attention, but she may not be sure what the "no" refers to. A better approach when she's barking is to say "come!" and reward her when she does. The positive command is as effective—and probably more so—than the negative one because it gives your dog a clearer sense of what you want her to do.

Use the right tone of voice. Dogs are extremely sensitive to even the smallest sounds or variations in sound. This means that the tone of your voice can make all the difference between whether a command is right or wrong.

In most situations, a firm, matter-of-fact tone is best because it sounds authoritative without being harsh or stern. However, sometimes dogs may be reluctant to obey. For instance, when they're tearing around the park with other dogs, they may not want to come to you. You need to persuade them that coming to you is as much fun as frolicking with their friends—so use a high-pitched, enthusiastic tone of voice that makes them really want to leave their friends for you.

There's one sure-fire method for recalling lagging pooches, says Shirley Sullivan, president of PR Dog, a training and dog day care center in Falls Church, Virginia. The formula is to say your dog's name, then tell her, "come here!" The word "here" should be said in a high-pitched, even falsetto tone of voice. Dogs called in this way respond eagerly. They hurry to their owners—and their tails are wagging.

Be consistent. Even though dogs can recognize the sounds of certain words, they don't necessarily understand their meaning. Using the same commands all the time is the only way to avoid confusion. When you tell your dog "off the chair" today and "get down" tomorrow, she won't have the slightest idea what you're trying to say.

No matter what commands you use—and ultimately the words themselves don't matter all that much—using them consistently will make them much more effective.

CHAPTER TWENTY-THREE

TALKING WITH HAND SIGNALS

Dogs take many of their cues from watching people and
responding to their body language. That's why hand signals
are a very effective way to communicate.

Three-year-old Cory, a Shetland sheepdog
from Vienna, Virginia, loved it when the
people in his family used the telephone.
As soon as they got on the horn, Cory would
bark, yodel, whine, and generally add his two
cents' worth to the conversation.

Unfortunately for Cory, his owners didn't
appreciate his ear-splitting contributions. So
they figured out how to stop his interruptions—
without saying a word to him. Their secret:
Hand signals.

These days, when Cory comes running at the
sound of the telephone, whoever answers it
responds with a hand signal that tells him to sit,
a signal Cory instantly responds to. If he opens
his mouth to start barking, a finger to the
person's lips quiets him immediately.

Cory's family has discovered one use for
hand signals. However, there are plenty of other
reasons why it's a good idea to use your hands to
communicate with your dog.

The Benefits of Hand Signals

It's often easier to teach a dog to respond to
hand signals than to verbal commands. "Dogs
are much more tuned in to body language than
to verbal communication," explains Pat Miller,

a trainer in Salinas, California. "It's actually
more challenging to teach a dog a word than
body language when training him."

For example, it doesn't take Miller much
time to use a treat and a hand signal to teach a
dog to lie down. "But even though you've been

*Hand signals are useful in noisy situations, such as
when this Staffordshire bull terrier and her owner
are pausing at a busy city street.*

using the word 'down' to teach the behavior, when you try using the word without the hand, your dog may not lie down. It takes a concerted effort to make a dog understand that the word alone is his cue to lie down," she says.

There are other situations in which a dog who responds to hand signals has a distinct advantage over one trained solely with verbal commands. For example:

• **When there's too much noise.** You can use hand signals to communicate with your dog in situations where it's not easy for him to hear you. For example, when your dog is within sight, but too far away for you to call him, a large, sweeping hand signal can tell him that it's time to head back to you.

Similarly, when you're on a noisy city street or on a beach with a booming surf, your dog's ability to understand your silent signals can help the two of you communicate. And when you want to communicate with your dog without making any noise—near someone who's asleep, for example—hand signals are just the ticket.

For dogs who are born deaf, like this blue merle Shetland sheepdog, hand signals can completely replace verbal commands.

• **When your dog is deaf.** Many dogs lose their hearing as they get older, says Shirley Sullivan, president of PR Dog, a training and dog day care center in Falls Church, Virginia. "By teaching your dog hand signals when he's young, he'll be accustomed to responding to hand signals if he goes deaf later in life. You won't have to start training him all over again."

Stan Chappell of Vienna, Virginia, has first-hand knowledge of how hand signals can help an aging dog. His poodle mix, Molly, lost her hearing when she was 14 years old. Because Chappell's wife had trained Molly with both voice and hand signals, Molly continued to obey commands and even learned new ones, despite her advanced age.

"I think Molly's ability to understand hand signals gave her more confidence," Chappell

BREED SPECIFIC

Some breeds are prone to being born deaf. The two genes that produce white or blue merle coloring in some dogs, such as collies, Australian shepherds, and bull terriers, are linked to a higher rate of deafness. Dalmatians have both these genes and also the highest rate of deafness: 30 percent are totally deaf.

says. "And because we could still communicate with her, I think the hand signals actually helped prolong her life."

When Hands Give the Wrong Message

Although there aren't any human hand signals or motions that are likely to rile a dog, like a canine equivalent of a rude gesture, some things people do with their hands can trigger negative reactions, especially from dogs who are shy, aggressive, or nervous.

For example, approaching a strange dog and reaching down to pet the top of his head may cause him to shy away or snap. In human terms, it's like having a stranger grab the back of your

This Rottweiler is more likely to accept a new person if she lets him sniff her outstretched arm and hand before she tries to pet him.

neck. Just as a person would find that upsetting and invasive, so does a dog.

Miller suggests letting a dog sniff your outstretched arm and hand before trying to pet him. "It's just proper canine etiquette," she explains. "When strange dogs greet each other, they sniff first before they romp and play. The socially inept dog who tries to run up and pounce playfully on another dog before a proper greeting often gets roundly trounced. It's like meeting a total stranger and hugging him instead of shaking hands."

In fact, any sudden moves with your hands or other parts of your body can startle or scare a dog, Miller says, even when they're not directed at him. "Dogs interpret everything around them in relation to themselves. Any motion that you make in the vicinity of a dog has meaning to that dog, such as slapping your buddy on the back or hugging your girlfriend. A dog may misinterpret such an action as a threat to his owner, and so think that he needs to protect her."

Training with Hand Signals

You can reinforce training with hand signals, especially if you're using treats or rewards to train your dog, says Miller. With a combination of hand signals and treats, you can coax the behavior you want from your dog, and then reward him for it. "And the more often a dog is rewarded for a particular behavior, the sooner he'll choose to offer that behavior," Miller says.

Hand signals also reinforce verbal commands—and when a dog learns to link a hand signal with a particular action, he'll soon respond to the hand signal alone.

COMMON HAND SIGNALS AND HOW TO TEACH THEM

Your dog doesn't need to be fluent in sign language to learn how to respond to common hand signals. Most dogs can learn basic signals in a matter of minutes.

Teach Your Dog to Stay

1 While your dog's sitting or lying down, show him the flat of your palm, with your fingertips pointed up. Move back one step, return immediately, praise your dog, and give a reward.

2 Repeat, but move two steps back this time. Slowly increase your distance away from your dog, and the length of time he must stay. Slowly increase the distractions in his environment, too, such as background noise and people moving around.

Teach Your Dog to Lie Down

1 Put your dog in a sitting position. Hold a treat in front of his face. Move your hand down to the ground and back toward you a few inches. The path your hand follows should be an L–shape.

2 As your dog follows your hand with his eyes, he will lie down. When he does, reward him with the treat and lots of praise.

Teach Your Dog to Sit

1 Find a reward for your dog, such as a small treat. After getting his attention and showing him the reward in your hand, move your hand up and over his head.

2 As he follows your hand with his eyes, his rear will drift toward the ground and he will automatically sit. When he has completed the sit, praise him lavishly and give him the reward.

Teach Your Dog to Come

1 Start by facing your dog, who should be a few feet away. Have your hands at your sides and a treat in your hand. Say your dog's name and the word "come." As you say "come," sweep your arm up and out to the side.

2 Then sweep your arm forward and into your chest. If your dog doesn't respond to the hand signal and verbal command, use the treat to lure him to you.

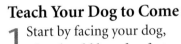

CHAPTER TWENTY-FOUR

TALKING WITH TOUCH

Dogs are experts at using their sense of touch to communicate with other dogs and people. Once we learn the different ways dogs like to be touched and what they mean, we, too, can be fluent in the language of touch.

Dogs depend on touch to a degree humans can barely comprehend. More than vision, scent, and hearing, touching allows them to form emotional bonds and communicate their most basic needs. Newborn puppies nudge their mom's nipples with their noses and paws to stimulate the flow of milk. Even when they're dozing, they get uneasy when she moves away and will only relax when they're touching once again.

Just as humans develop language skills early in life, dogs quickly become adept in the language of touch. Throughout their lives, in fact, their interactions with other dogs and with people resemble a contact sport. To us, it all looks like play. But to dogs, a hip nudge, nose bump, or paw push speaks as clearly as a shout.

The Meaning of Touch

Dogs spend a lot of time sorting out their respective roles, and they use touch as a way of establishing control or subordinance. When two dogs meet, one dog may push the other with his shoulder. It looks like a playful nudge—and in some cases it is—but it's also a way of saying, "I can push you around so you'd better toe the line." A push with the nose is another way of communicating authority. Dogs who are shy and retiring will rarely use these types of touch, while dogs who are naturally dominant use them all the time.

Their social interactions aren't all about status, of course. Dogs love to play, and once the "Who's in charge?" preliminaries are out of the

From the moment they're born, puppies, such as these Saint Bernards, begin to communicate by touch. The mother and the young pups only relax when they're touching.

way, they'll use a variety of touches to communicate their willingness—or their reluctance—to have a good time.

Some of the signals a dog uses to establish status, like putting his paws on another dog's shoulders or banging him with his hips, are also friendly overtures. A dog who pushes with his nose, for example, and is also wagging his tail or bowing his front end, is saying he'd like to play. Even touches that look ominous, like grabbing the fur around the neck, may be friendly as long as the dogs know each other and they're displaying other play signals at the same time.

There's no way to know for sure what a dog is trying to communicate just by looking at touch signals. You have to look at the whole picture: how he's moving, whether he has a smile on his face, how his tail is wagging, and so on. By licking, a dog can be asking for attention, showing affection, or being submissive, says Robin Kovary, director of the American Dog Trainers Network in New York City. If in the past your dog's nuzzling of your hand has brought him friendly pats from you, he's likely to nuzzle you whenever he wants affection. If you give your dog a treat whenever he nuzzles your hand, you can bet that future nuzzles will be your dog's way of hitting you up for a snack.

Touching Back

Dogs grow up "speaking" touch, but for people, learning to communicate with touch is like mastering a second language. Fortunately, dogs are patient. They understand that people are a little slow sometimes, and they will execute an entire chorus of touches to make their point.

This retriever mix is using a signal of dominance by putting his legs on the shoulders of his companion, but his wagging tail shows that he's only playing.

Suppose a dog is in the mood for attention. Were he with another dog, he'd nudge him a few times and wag his tail, and all would be understood. But he knows from experience that the subtleties of touch get lost in the translation from dog to human. So he'll do the canine equivalent of talking louder. A hand lick may be followed by a nose nudge. Or he'll rub against your legs and put his head on your knee. He knows that sooner or later you'll look up from the paper, notice he's there, and give him a pleasant rubdown, or, if he's really lucky, something to eat. Over time, he'll learn which types of touch you're most likely to understand and will start with those. He'll also learn that different people in the family respond to different kinds of touches.

While dogs are pretty good at telling their owners what they want, people aren't as fluent. They assume that touches that mean something

151

to them, like a head rub or a big hug, will also mean something to their dogs. Most of the time, however, the result is pure confusion. People shake hands when they meet, for example, but dogs hate having their feet touched. We put our hands on each other's shoulders to express affection, while dogs may view this type of touch as a threat.

It's not difficult to learn the language of touch. Even though dogs respond to dozens of touches, you can communicate most messages with just a few different kinds. Here are the main ones.

• **Don't be afraid.** Dogs usually greet each other by ducking their heads and keeping their bodies fairly low to the ground. They do this because a dog who stands tall may be issuing a challenge. This is where confusion sets in. People are a lot taller than dogs. In their eyes, we look pretty formidable. And because we're tall, we tend to reach down and pet their highest part, the top of the head. Among dogs, touching the top of the head is a clear signal that they're being challenged.

The best way to reassure dogs is to change our greetings. In addition to stooping down, it's a good idea to touch them under the chin or on the chest instead of on the head. "It's less intimidating than a pat on the head, which some dogs dislike," says Kovary.

• **Take it easy.** Whenever your dog is showing signs of stress—because he's being groomed, for example, or he's figured out that you and he are headed for the vet—make him lie down, then place your hand on his groin, which will calm him down, advises Kovary. Stroking a dog's side or chest slowly and firmly is also calming—in mature dogs, it's known to reduce heart rate and lower blood pressure.

• **I like what you're doing.** Since dogs crave physical contact, virtually any touch will let them know that you're happy with what they're doing. "When my dog is lying down quietly and not barking, I use touch as a form of praise to reinforce a behavior I like," says Sandy Myers, director of Narnia Pet Training in Naperville, Illinois. Gently pulling your dog's ears or rubbing his belly will let him know that you're pretty happy with him.

This German shepherd knows that he's not being issued a challenge when his owner gets down to his level to greet him. He is also reassured by the strokes under the chin.

Most dogs dislike being touched on the paws and will try to pull away. You can get them used to it by touching their paws when they're young.

Touches to Avoid

It's pretty hard to annoy a dog who spends his whole life looking up to you and who enjoys nothing more than some of your attention. But owners often forget that what feels good to them doesn't necessarily feel good to their dogs. Dogs view some kinds of touch, no matter how gentle or kindly intended, in all the wrong ways.

Most dogs hate having their feet touched. Experts aren't sure why it bothers them. It's possible they have ticklish feet and the touching makes them uncomfortable. Dogs rarely touch each other's feet, and in the canine book of manners, it's probably considered an unacceptable liberty, says Pat Miller, a dog trainer and behaviorist in Salinas, California.

Hugging is another kind of touch dogs wish humans would keep to themselves. The closest dogs come to hugging is when mothers carry puppies around in their mouths. Apart from that, dogs don't use clingy behavior to express affection. In fact, hugging probably reminds them, unconsciously, of the days when a close "embrace" meant they were being attacked. It's also possible that dogs associate hugging with being mounted by a dominant dog. Hugs restrict a dog's ability to move or escape, and they're not happy about that, says Kovary.

That's why you shouldn't discipline your dog by holding your hands on either side of his head—it's a gesture that makes him uncomfortable because he feels locked in.

A HAIRY BUSINESS

The sense of touch is very important to dogs, but they lose some of that sensitivity because their hairy coats essentially insulate them from things in the environment. To compensate, they're equipped with specialized touch receptors that allow them to pick up subtle messages.

These receptors are sensory hairs, called vibrissae, which are embedded in areas of the skin that have concentrated blood supplies and numerous nerve endings. The vibrissae are located above the eyes, below the jaws, and on the muzzle. Dogs use these touch-sensitive hairs to find out more about their environment, such as the strength and direction of air currents and the texture and shape of objects.

CHAPTER TWENTY-FIVE

TALKING WITH SCENTS

A dog's most powerful sense is the sense of smell. They use it to
find out all manner of fascinating things about the world and
to communicate with other dogs they encounter.

Dogs have an astonishing sense of smell. Researchers have found, in fact, that dogs are up to a million times more sensitive to certain scents, such as sweat, than humans are. So it's not surprising that they do much of their communicating by scent. Watch your dog closely the next time you take a walk. You'll see he spends relatively little time looking around because most of his attention is, quite literally, right in front of his nose.

This explains why even well-trained dogs will sometimes lunge, nose-first, toward a fire hydrant, tree, or other object of interest. Your dog's nose is so sensitive he can smell traces of other dogs that are hours or even days old, and he can discover their sex, their attitude, even their seniority just by taking a sniff. Essentially, he can "talk" to other dogs simply by smelling their scent—or by leaving his own.

A dog's instinctive need to sniff and be sniffed can be irritating for dog-walkers in a hurry, but it provides a valuable teaching tool. Since dogs use scent to talk to each other, it's possible for humans to use scents to talk to their dogs.

Putting Them at Ease

Dogs are creatures of habit who don't always like changes in their routine or lifestyle. You can use scents to help them deal with new or difficult situations more easily, says Robin Kovary, director of the American Dog Trainers Network in New York City. When you board your dog, for example, you can help him adjust by leaving one of your old, unwashed T-shirts or other

*When his owner goes away and leaves this beagle
with friends, he also leaves behind a piece of his
clothing. A familiar scent helps comfort dogs and
makes them feel more secure.*

Why do dogs roll in stinky things?

Dogs have many endearing features, but rolling in smelly substances isn't one of them. Unfortunately, it's almost impossible to make them stop. Whether they're walking on a horse trail or exploring the neighborhood on trash day, they love nothing better than finding a nasty bit of business and rolling in it.

It may strike humans as an unpleasant habit, but it makes perfect sense to dogs, says Sharon Crowell-Davis, D.V.M., coordinator of the Applied Animal Behavior program at the University of Georgia in Athens. "A wild dog that's hunting doesn't want to smell like a dog, but like his prey," she explains. "So he rolls in dung or on a carcass in an effort to control what he smells like."

Of course, dogs today don't hunt anything more formidable than a bowl of food on the kitchen floor. But in their minds, it pays to smell right and be ready—just in case.

garments. He will feel less frightened and insecure because your scent will keep him company.

Just as dogs get nervous about new situations, they're sometimes nervous about new people, too. That's why trainers recommend introducing dogs to new arrivals in the family—a new baby, for example—by letting them sniff a blanket or an article of clothing belonging to the person before they meet face to face. Dogs who "meet" people by first getting to know their scent will feel as though they've been properly introduced and will be more likely to accept them and will not be alarmed when they meet.

Teaching with Scents

Just as dogs use their noses to discover good things—like cookies on a counter—they also depend on scent to warn them away from things that aren't so good. You can combine scents with other training techniques to help dogs learn what they shouldn't do, says Shirley Sullivan, president of PR Dog, a training and dog day care center in Falls Church, Virginia.

For instance, you can discourage your dog from pilfering food off the counter by sprinkling the area with a distinctive scent such as anise oil, while also booby-trapping the area by lining tin cans along the edge of the counter. The next time he makes a raid, the cans will tumble down and startle him. Because dogs depend so much on smell, he'll associate the smell of the anise oil with the frightening noise. After a while, the oil alone will be enough to deter him, Sullivan says.

Smells that dogs find unpleasant can also help them learn. For example, citronella collars can help to stop dogs barking. The quick burst of citronella that's released with the first or second woof will soon persuade a dog that being quiet is better than getting a noseful of a nasty smell. You can also use citronella to keep dogs off the furniture or out of the trash.

It's not only smells that send messages, but also the lack of smells. For example, dogs that have urinated in the house will sometimes return to the same place, drawn by the lingering odor. That's why you need to remove not only the stain, but also the odor. Odor neutralizers, available in pet supply stores, do the job quickly and easily. Once the smell is gone, he'll be much less likely to return to that spot in the future.

CHAPTER TWENTY-SIX

TALKING WITH SOUND

Even when they're sound asleep, dogs always keep one ear open.
They rely on their hearing much more than humans do, so using sound
is a very effective way to communicate.

Dogs hear much better than we do. They can hear sounds from four times farther away, and they can also hear high-pitched sounds that are way beyond our range of hearing. Their sensitivity to sounds is important because they rely on their hearing more than we do. When we talk to our dogs, they don't merely listen to our words. They also focus on the way our voices sound.

And they listen to a lot more than just our voices. The rattle of kibble in the bag, the creak of a step outside the front door, or the opening of the drawer where the leash is kept are just a few of the sounds that tell dogs that something's about to happen. "Most of the time we're teaching our dogs things whether we realize it or not, because dogs are always looking for and interpreting clues about what's happening in their environment," says Pat Miller, a trainer in Salinas, California.

Because dogs are inquisitive creatures who like to learn, we can take advantage of their curiosity by using their keen hearing to communicate the messages we want them to hear.

This Australian shepherd fetches her leash whenever her owner jingles her house keys because she knows that's the signal that she's going for a walk.

Basic Vocabulary

Nearly all dog owners talk with their pets—not just when they're giving commands or praise, but also to share their feelings or to point out an exciting sight, such as "Do you see the ball over there?"

No one knows for sure how much human language dogs really understand. Highly trained show dogs understand dozens of commands,

and nearly every dog knows at least a few key words, like "walk" and "dinner," as well as a few more complex phrases. "Most people can teach their dogs 5 to 10 words, or more if they try hard enough," says Sharon Crowell-Davis, D.V.M, coordinator of the Applied Animal Behavior program at the University of Georgia in Athens.

This shiba inu can tell from her owner's happy tone of voice that she's pleased with her.

Five or 10 words may not sound like a lot, but they pretty much cover the commands most dogs need to know—like "sit," "come," "down," and "stay." However, dogs focus on more than just commands. They listen and make associations every time we speak. And they're pretty good at putting things together.

Even though a dog may not completely understand a relatively complex (to her) phrase such as "get the ball," experience will teach her what you're trying to communicate and soon she won't have any trouble catching your drift. It won't be long before she responds by rooting through her toy basket in search of her ball.

Dogs also tune into sounds that we don't think twice about. Miller's computer, for example, says "good-bye" whenever she logs off. Her dogs may not understand the words, but they've learned that "good-bye" means that Miller's finished working and will soon let them go outside to play.

Dogs don't attach meanings to words in the same way that people do, so you can't expect them to expand their vocabulary right away, says Robin Kovary, director of the American Dog Trainers Network in New York City. They have to hear the same word or phrase at least a few times before it takes on meaning. However, if that word or phrase becomes associated with something they like, such as a walk, they'll make the connection fairly quickly.

Suppose you want your dog to know what "walk" means. Once or twice a day, say "walk!" as you pick up the leash before going outside, and make sure your dog sees and hears what you're doing. It won't take her long to learn exactly what "walk!" means—and she'll demonstrate her knowledge with tail-wagging, jumping-around excitement. You can do the same thing with words and phrases like "eat," "ball," or "come here." As school teachers can attest, repetition followed by fun is the best way to teach the basics.

Of course, no matter how many words your dog learns, she'll never understand their "meaning" in the same way that you do. But she'll understand other aspects of words, like their sound and inflection. In other words, to

157

talk effectively with dogs, we need to focus not just on what we say, but also on how we say it.

Talking with Tone

Since dogs are acutely aware of the subtlest of sounds, they're very sensitive to your tone of voice. In fact, trainers believe that your tone of voice is more important than the words you use when you're communicating with dogs.

You can put this to the test simply by telling your dog that she's the most miserable, good-for-nothing cur that ever walked the earth. As long as you talk in a happy-sounding tone of voice, she'll wag her tail and wriggle her body in delight.

Conversely, telling a dog how wonderful she is while using a stern, low-pitched voice will make her a little nervous. Her ears may go back, her tail will curl downward, and she'll try to make herself as small as possible. She'll be unhappy and worried that she's displeased you because she recognizes the tone you use when you're unhappy with her.

Most trainers recommend using three different tones of voice when working with dogs. For commands, use a firm but even tone of voice. For praise, a happy, relatively high-pitched tone works best. For corrections, use a low-pitched, disapproving tone.

These tones are effective because they mimic the tones that dogs make when communicating with each other. Speaking in an even voice, for example, is similar to the pitch of a dog's everyday bark, which is why it's ideal for commands and other matter-of-fact messages. A high-pitched tone of voice resembles a dog's excited bark, so it's a good way to convey happiness and pleasure. And low-pitched, stern voices resemble the growl of disapproval from a mother dog, and that's why it's the best tone for giving corrections.

It's not always easy, of course, for people to vary their voices enough to capture the full range of dog attention. Men with deep voices may have trouble raising their voices high enough to convey praise and pleasure in a way that dogs can easily understand, says Greg Strong, a trainer in Easton, Maryland. Women with high voices may have the opposite challenge: Lowering their pitch sufficiently to correct their pets. Not surprisingly, many men are better at giving corrections, and many women are better at giving praise.

For both men and women, the most important thing is to make sure that your tone of voice matches the message you're trying to convey. "I've heard people tell a dog to sit, but then they put a kind of question mark at the end, like they're asking the dog to sit instead of telling her to," says Strong. If you do that, your dog may not obey—because she may not realize you've given her a command.

Beyond Words

The fact that dogs depend on sounds and not merely words to understand the world around them is something you can use to your advantage, both for training and simply to communicate a little more effectively.

Suppose you don't want your dog to beg while you're eating dinner. One way to send that message to your dog is to tell her "off!" or "no

Listening for a Living

For some dogs, tuning in to everyday sounds isn't just an adventure—it's their job, and they can make a world of difference for people who have lost some or all of their hearing.

Called hearing dogs, these are intelligent, eager-to-please canines who have been trained to alert their owners when they hear door bells, smoke alarms, telephones, and alarm clocks. The dogs can even be trained to alert parents that their baby is crying, says Joyce Fehl, director of development at National Education for Assistance Dog Services in Princeton, Massachusetts.

Most of the dogs trained by her organization are adopted from animal shelters, and they're screened to determine how well they can recognize and react to certain sounds, Fehl explains. A standard test is to set off an alarm clock. If a dog runs to the clock, proving she can identify where the sound is coming from, she's a good candidate for further training.

All the dogs are taught to recognize certain sounds, but they're also capable of learning new sounds once they've been adopted by their new owners. Barbara Spano of Carteret, New Jersey, discovered this for herself one morning when her hearing dog, a poodle named Lilly, pawed insistently at her face to wake her up.

When Barbara got out of bed she felt the floor vibrating. She looked out the window and saw that a truck had crashed into the utility pole by her house. She called 911, and the emergency officers later said she was lucky that her house hadn't caught fire—all of the electrical lines had been pulled away from the wall.

Hearing dogs are encouraged to think independently and they receive extensive training. But the one trait that makes them special is that they have very deep attachments to their owners and will do everything possible to keep them safe. "They also need to sleep with one ear open," Fehl adds.

message—and eventually she'll learn that throat-clearing means hand-outs won't be forthcoming and that it's time to go away.

The fact that dogs can learn to attach meanings to all kinds of verbal sounds has also led to the use of a technique called clicker training.

A clicker is a small plastic box with a metal strip that makes a clicking sound when pushed and released. When a dog obeys a command, the trainer or owner clicks the clicker instead of saying, "Good dog!" Immediately after the click, the dog gets a treat. "Clicker training is a good idea because it works with the dog's mind rather than against it," says Miller. That's because it uses positive reinforcement and rewards a dog instantly for obeying.

You can achieve the same effect on your dog with other sounds, too. Any sound that dogs associate with praise and pleasure, such as an enthusiastic "yes!" or a quick hand clap, will work just as well.

The idea is to use sounds that your dog recognizes that tell her that she's done something right the instant that she's done so. This will help your dog learn faster, and you'll both enjoy being able to communicate a little bit better.

begging." Or you can simply clear your throat and look directly at her. The noise will get her attention, and your stare will tell her that you're not pleased. It won't take her long to get the

CHAPTER TWENTY-SEVEN

TALKING WITH TREATS

Just like humans, dogs enjoy good things to eat.
But treats aren't just for fun—they can also help you
communicate better with your dog.

Dogs are distractable creatures with short attention spans, which is why it's not always easy to get them to notice what you're saying. But they're also capable of intense concentration, especially when food is involved. That's why many trainers recommend using treats to help us communicate better with our dogs. Whether you're training your dog, distracting him from bad behavior, or looking for ways to keep him amused, nothing speaks louder than food.

Trainers often use treats, such as cheese, freeze-dried liver, or other tasty goodies, as incentives for good behavior and to keep dogs focused during training sessions, says Robin Kovary, director of the American Dog Trainers Network in New York City. More is involved than the fact that most dogs have insatiable appetites. Of all your dog's senses, the sense of smell is the most powerful— more powerful by far than his sense of hearing or eyesight. When you're teaching basic obedi-

During training, a tasty treat helps keep this fox terrier's attention focused.

ence, words like "come" or "sit" don't have a lot of meaning, at least at first. But an odoriferous dog biscuit sends a message they can understand right away. Combining two messages—a verbal command coupled with a more compelling scent—makes training a whole lot easier.

Suppose, for example, that you're teaching your dog to come when you call. At first he won't understand the word "come." And he'll have a hard time paying attention to what you're saying because he'll probably be distracted by everything else that's going on around him, from the smell of the grass to a fly buzzing past. But when you're holding a treat, his attention will be riveted. Just as important, he'll be intensely motivated to do whatever it takes to gain that treat. So the treat helps in two ways: It helps him focus, and it rewards him when he comes galloping over.

The same technique works when you're trying to teach your dog to stay. The "stay" command is one of the hardest to teach because it involves leaving your dog in one place while you go someplace else. After about five seconds, dogs start getting bored just sitting or lying there, and they start looking around for distractions. That's usually when training sessions turn into chasing sessions.

Everything changes when you put a tasty treat on the ground a few feet in front of him, says Shirley Sullivan, president of PR Dog, a training and dog day care center in Falls Church, Virginia. It's as though all of the distractions were suddenly obliterated. Rather than desperately wanting to get out of school, your dog can hardly wait to do what you want—as long as he gets something to eat when he does it.

Of course, if you give your dog a treat every time he does something right, you'll not only have a well-behaved dog, but also a fat one. When you're training a puppy or giving a refresher course to an adult, treats are a great way to keep him focused and motivated. But good things should be given in moderation. "You don't want your dog to become fixated on food," Kovary says. Once your dog has learned the basics, he really doesn't need the extra incentives. Of course, humans don't need ice cream, either, but we appreciate having treats now and then—and your dog does, too.

The Power of Distraction

Treats send other messages besides "sit" or "stay." You can also use them to distract your dog from doing things you'd rather he didn't, like struggling when you brush his coat or barking out the window at butterflies. Treats are

especially good for problem behaviors such as barking, if only because dogs can't eat and bark at the same time.

Or suppose you're trying to stop your dog from chasing cars. While walking your dog on a leash, have a treat ready when you hear a car approach. Quickly use the treat to coax your dog into a sitting position—and keep him focused on the treat so that he holds that position as the car goes by. You're helping your dog replace a bad habit with the behavior you want, and treats can help speed up that process, Sullivan says. After a while, he'll be so used to ignoring cars that he'll do it automatically, even when you've phased out the treats.

You can also use treats to keep your dog happy when you're away from home. This is important because dogs who are left alone often get bored or anxious and express their feelings by barking constantly, digging, or chewing. Something as simple as giving your dog a treat-stuffed toy, using a Kong, a Buster Cube, or a hollow bone, can often be enough to solve the problem. Because when a dog has a job to do—ferreting out tasty goodies—he will be too occupied to be anxious or bored.

A rubber toy filled with treats provides this Samoyed with a lot of fun and mental stimulation.

Credits and Acknowledgments

(t=top, b=bottom, l=left, r=right, c=center, F=front, C=cover, B=back).
All photographs are copyright to the sources listed below.

PHOTOGRAPH CREDITS

Ad-Libitum: Stuart Bowey, ic, vib, viic, 5t, 9c, 13b, 20t, 20b, 26t, 30b, 35tl, 38t, 40b, 42b, 48b, 49b, 50b, 51b, 51tr, 52br, 55b, 57t, 59tr, 62t, 66b, 68t, 70b, 71br, 72tr, 73br, 78tr, 79b, 80b, 82bl, 82br, 83bl, 83bc, 83br, 84bl, 85tl, 86b, 87t, 87c, 87b, 88t, 88c, 88b, 92b, 93br, 95b, 97b, 98b, 103t, 107bl, 107br, 109t, 111b, 112t, 116t, 117b, 120b, 122b, 124t, 128b, 134t, 136bl, 137br, 140bl, 140br, 141t, 142b, 144t, 145b, 147b, 150b, 157t, 160t, BCb.

Auscape International: Français-COGIS, 27b, 53tr, 110t, 118t; Gissey/COGIS, 56b; Hermeline/COGIS, 71tl, 94t, 108b, 153t; Jean-Michel Labat, 25t; Labat-COGIS, 17b, 32c, 54tl, 90t; Labat/Lanceau, 60t, 93tr; Labat/Lanceau/COGIS, 64t; Lanceau-COGIS, 47t, 89b, 152b; Varin/Cogis, 44c.

André Martin: 91tr.

Australian Picture Library: Philip Reeson 39c.

Behling & Johnson: Norvia Behling, 12t, 24b, 58b, 72bl, 80tl, 156b.

Bill Bachman and Associates: 85bl, 102b.

Bruce Coleman Ltd: Adriano Bacchella, 23b, 99tr; Jorg and Petra Wegner, 74b, 106t.

Dale C. Spartas: 10t, 14t, 37tr, 59bl, 63b, 78bl, 91bl, 115t, 130c, 138t, BCcl.

FLPA: Gerard Lacz, 54bl, 79tl.

Foto Natura: Klein/Hubert, 74tr.

Graham Meadows Photography: viiib, 2t, 53bl, 73tl, 127t, 129t, 136tr.

Judith E. Strom: 6b, 146t.

Kent and Donna Dannen: 37b, 46b, 52tl, 105b, 123t, 132b, 161b, BCtr.

NHPA: Susanne Danegger, 125b.

Oxford Scientific Film: John Mitchell, 35br.

R. T. Wilbie Animal Photography: 34t.

Rodale Images: Mitch Mandel, iic, 41t, 85c, 126b, BCcr.

Ron Kimball Photography: xc, 28b, 74b, 81b, 84t, 100c, BCtl, FC © 1993.

Ron Levy: 29c.

Stock Photos: Anthony Edgeworth, 113b.

The Image Bank: Vikki Hart, 15b. Dag Sundberg, 39c; Sobel/Klonsh, 151t.

The Photo Library: 119b, Brian Stablyk, 67t; Gordon E Smith, 154b; Lorentz Gullachsen, 92tl; Tim Davis, 143t.

Yves Lanceau/Auscape: 8t.

ILLUSTRATION CREDITS

Chris Wilson, 65b, 148,149

The publisher would like to thank the following people for their assistance in the preparation of this book:
Trudie Craig, Peta Gorman, Tracey Jackson.

Special thanks to the following people who kindly brought their dogs in for photo shoots:
Len Antcliff and "Bozie"; Kathy Ash and "Max"; Leigh Audette and "Boss"; Tim and Andrea Barnard and "Sam", "Rigel", "Tessa", and "Molly"; Anne Bateman and "Bonnie"; Esther Blank and "Max"; Corinne Braye and "Minne"; Sophie and Joel Cape and "Max" and "Millie"; Matt Gavin-Wear and "Amber"; Robyn Hayes and "Patsy"; Anne Holmes and "Marli"; Sophie Holsman and "Zane"; Fran Johnston and "Tess"; Suzie Kennedy and "Eddie"; Natalie Kidd and "Cisco"; Michael Lenton and "Jasper"; Gish Lesh and "Twister"; Lubasha Macdonald and "Tigra"; David McGregor and "Kelly"; Cameron McFarlane and "Donald"; Chris Wilson and "Julia".

Index